SHADES OF THE
ALHAMBRA

There is nothing more cruel in life than to be blind in Granada.
On the wall of the Garden of the Adarves, the Alhambra

1. *The Alhambra gardens*

SHADES OF THE
ALHAMBRA

Raleigh Trevelyan

LONDON
The Folio Society
1984

*Set in twelve point Linotron Bembo, one
point leaded, by Deltatype, Ellesmere Port. Printed
by Springbourne Press on Rapier Matt cartridge and bound
by R. J. Acford.*

FOR RAUL

I am grateful to the following for their assistance in the early stages of my researches: M. and Mme Amahan, Raúl Balín Rodriguez, Roger Boase, Isabel Cajide, Darío Cabanelas Rodriguez O.F.M., Victoriano del Cerro Bex, Abdelkader Erzini, Sir Brinsley Ford, Antonio Fernández-Puertas, María de los Santos García Felguera, Excmo Emilio García Gómez, Leslie T. Phillips, Juan de Dios López González, Juan Moll, José Manuel Monroy Balín, María Angustias Moreno Olmedo, Margarita de Pedroso y Sturdza, Joaquín and Carmen Prieto-Moreno, Francisco Prieto-Moreno y Pardo, Laura de los Ríos de García Lorca, Michael Scott, Juan Zozaya Stabel-Hansen. My thanks also to Dr Richard Hitchcock for reading the manuscript.

CONTENTS

Editorial Note

Mudéjares	*Muslims under Christian rule*
Mozárabes	*Christians under Muslim rule*
Renegados	*Christians turned Muslim*
Moriscos	*Muslims turned Christian*

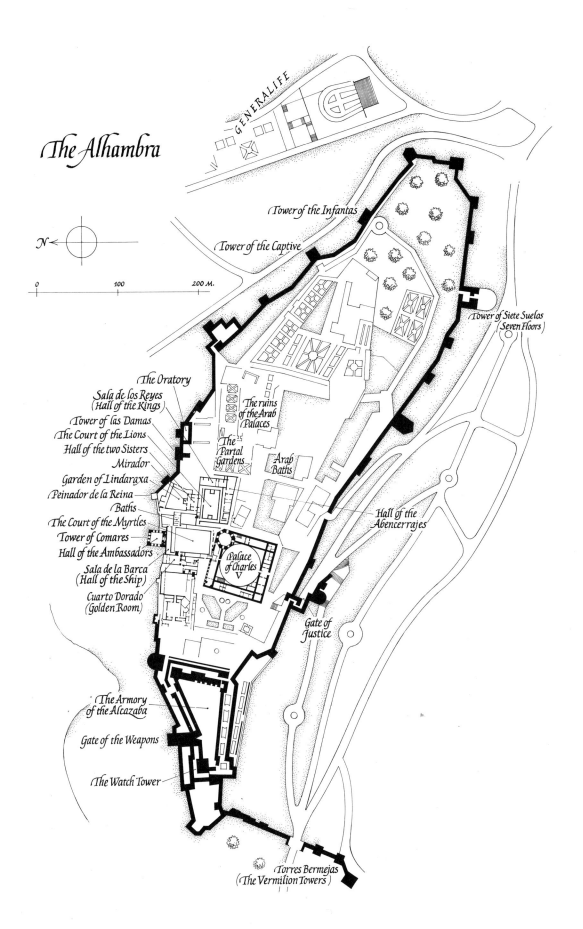

The Alhambra

GENERALIFE

N ←

0   100   200 M.

Tower of the Infantas

Tower of the Captive

Tower of Siete Suelos
(Seven Floors)

The Oratory

Sala de los Reyes
(Hall of the Kings)

Tower of las Damas

The Court of the Lions

Hall of the two Sisters

Mirador

Garden of Lindaraxa

Peinador de la Reina

Baths

The Court of the Myrtles

Tower of Comares

Hall of the Ambassadors

Sala de la Barca
(Hall of the Ship)

Cuarto Dorado
(Golden Room)

The ruins
of the Arab
Palaces

The
Partal
Gardens

Arab
Baths

Palace
of Charles
V

Hall of the
Abencerrajes

Gate of
Justice

The Armory
of the Alcazaba

Gate of the Weapons

The Watch Tower

Torres Bermejas
(The Vermilion Towers)

PREFACE

I was in the Tower of the Infantas, at the farthest end of the Alhambra's battlements and away from the main flood of tourists. Across the bed of a small valley, perhaps once used as a moat, were the cypresses of the Generalife gardens –cypresses as old as Zoraïde, Washington Irving had said. To the left I could see the terracotta roofs of the Albaicín and the hill of the Sacromonte, with its gypsy caves among prickly pears. Beyond, under the high transparent sky, was the long pale range of the sierras, the boundary of the old Muslim kingdom of Granada. I could smell jasmine, and now and then a late nightingale would sing.

The author of my guidebook was rather scornful about the Tower of the Infantas, saying that it showed only too clearly the decadence of Nasrid art, as it dated – or at least its interior dated – from the reign of Muhammed VII, who died in 1408. I had to admit that it could not compare with the shimmering glory of the throne room of the Hall of the Ambassadors or the magic arcades of the Court of the Lions. Nor yet could it compete with its neighbour, the Tower of the Captive, which is indeed a masterpiece and has a superb stalactite ceiling of the time of Yusuf I, some seventy years earlier. The Tower of the Captive is in reality a small palace, whereas the Tower of the Infantas, although grand, is more domestic, a series of halls on several floors over a courtyard.

It is difficult not to pile on the hyperboles about the Alhambra, which has been described at various periods as evanescent, floating disembodied, sensuously exotic, luminous, a delicate cluster of soap-bubbles, a rose preserved in snow, domes of heaven, a kaleidoscope, a terrestrial paradise, a web of petrified lace, pearls in an emerald setting, and having an Aladdin gorgeousness. Victor Hugo wrote:

> *L'Alhambra! L'Alhambra! Palais que les Génies*
> *Ont doré comme un rêve et rempli d'harmonies.*

None of which, as it happens, and especially after seeing the Alhambra several times and in different lights and seasons (and this is important), seems all that exaggerated.

On a first visit, it is true, some people claim to find the impact overwhelming. Others may have attempted to search for comparisons in

2. General plan of the Alhambra

3. *A view of the Alhambra from the Tower of San Cristóbal. A drawing by Richard Ford, 1833*

style with Islamic buildings of the East, or have admired the architects' use of space, sky or water, and the geometric designs of the *azulejos* (tiles); or yet again they may have concentrated on the historical significance of the many poetic inscriptions around the walls or on the fountains. The Alhambra can be looked on as the last flowering of a brilliant civilization, which also produced the mosque of Córdoba and the Giralda of Seville, or it can be regarded as a classic fortress–city. But a feeling of mystery will always be the last, and lasting, impression, and for this inevitably one has to return to Washington Irving: 'The peculiar charm of this old dreamy palace is its power of calling up vague reveries and picturings of the past and thus clothing naked realities with the illusion of the memory and the imagination.'

Perhaps it was the nightingale that sent me into a vague reverie that afternoon in the Tower of the Infantas. Perhaps the crumbling brickwork outside, contrasting with the exotic interior of the building, made me think of the time of the Romantics, when apparently any stray traveller could take up lodgings in the Alhambra. I could almost see the figure of Washington Irving on his evening stroll up the 'glen', overshadowed 'by

8

fig-trees, pomegranates and myrtles', and looking up to spy a pretty 'young female', her head adorned with flowers.

The lucky Théophile Gautier was able to move his mattress from room to room around the Court of the Lions. Richard Ford's family was installed in the old Palace of the Partal whose arches are now reflected in the great pool guarded by two more lions, taken from the Maristán or Muslim hospital. I wouldn't have minded putting my mattress down in the Hall of the Two Sisters, the most beautiful of them all, or for that matter in the Hall of the Abencerrajes in spite of the gruesome legend about the beheadings. But I would also have been perfectly happy in the Tower of the Infantas, and would not have been at all disturbed by its ghost, the desolate princess bewailing her lost love (her own fault) and singing 'plaintive ditties'.

Richard Ford fulminated against the people of Granada for letting the Alhambra deteriorate. He and his contemporaries would hardly complain now about the state of the main buildings though they might regret the influx of tourists – for which they were in part responsible. Gone are the 'tatterdemalion' families who once were their inhabitants, along with gypsies and vagrants, and more homely characters like Irving's Mateo and Dolores. The Alhambra was plundered and desecrated over the centuries after the departure of the Muslims, restored at the end of the last century, and restored all over again in this. Yet the effect is still a kind of perfection.

The elegant pavilions of the Generalife, the old summer palace, Jinan al-Arif in Arabic, the garden of the architect or overseer, have been even more restored. Its marvellous gardens have been enlarged in recent years and include the open-air theatre for the International Festival that always begins at the end of June. With the hedged-in patios, vistas between cypresses, beds full of roses, magnolias, syringa and oleanders, and the vivacious gushing fountains and still pools with fish and waterlilies, the Generalife gardens capture the mood and tranquillity of one side of the two hundred and fifty years' rule of the Nasrid sultans.

In a sense there is a feeling of intrusion or even sadness as one 'loiters', to use a favourite word of Washington Irving's, through the Alhambra's halls, once crowded with courtiers and guards, its 'empty realities' now devoid of the rugs, silks, cushions and lustreware vessels that once would have furnished them. And yet, I thought, as I leant over the balustrade of the Tower of the Infantas and watched the mountains turn violet over the Sacromonte, the Alhambra lives. New archaeological discoveries are made and new theories about the past are thereby produced, nineteenth-century mistakes are mended, the gardens are replanted with shrubs and varieties of roses of which the Arabs would never have dreamt –

9

presumably in their day they only knew *rosa gallica* or *damascena* – and would never have seen such a sight as the plumbago now tumbling over the wall by the Infantas. Then there is the International Festival, with concerts in the Generalife and in the Court of the Myrtles. Even the sometimes maligned palace of Charles V, which on first impression seems to crush on the Moorish buildings but is nevertheless the most splendid piece of Renaissance architecture in Spain, has come into its own, housing the Alhambra museum and library, and with concerts in the great circular courtyard. As for the floodlighting, the effect from a distance is stunning, and would have amazed – or more likely alarmed – the soldiers of the Catholic Kings in the 1480s; the towers really do seem to float disembodied. For myself, I shall not forget, one floodlit night, the eerie strangeness of those twelve beasts supporting the ancient fountain in the Court of the Lions, or the translucence of the pools of the Partal garden, with frogs plopping off the waterlily leaves.

The festival in effect had its origin in a 'concourse' of *cante jondo* an early form of the modern flamenco, organized in 1922 by Manuel de Falla with Federico García Lorca and various Granada personalities. This was followed in 1923 with concerts of the music of Ravel and Stravinsky. *Cante jondo*, which means literally deep song and is typically Andalusian, though with origins in the East, possibly India, is full of the anguish of impossible love and the grief and tragedies of a people whose ancestors have seen so many persecutions, invasions and cruelty. Presumably Washington Irving was thinking of something more cheerful, and had the medieval troubadours in mind, when he wrote about his Christian cavaliers serenading the three captive Moorish infantas in the tower, with 'a Spanish roundelay to the accompaniment of the guitar'.

I had realized that a rehearsal for a concert would soon begin in the Generalife, and had watched the performers arriving along the cypress walk opposite. Now the Alhambra was about to be closed to tourists, and I could hear a warning bell. Having fallen into a slightly melancholy mood – or reverie – I thought of the murder of Lorca in the Civil War, near Viznár in the hills outside Granada, at a place called the Fuente Grande, which was known to the Muslims as Ainadamar, the Fountain of Tears. Falla had tried to intervene at the time of Lorca's arrest, and later had not had the courage to tell the family that his friend had already been shot.

The light was beginning to fail, and an orange glow appeared in the sky. Now the air was full of the excited screams of swifts. A *guardián* was insisting that I must leave, and as I walked away the scent of jasmine seemed stronger, the plumbago seemed brighter, and I heard the first notes of Falla's *La Vida Breve* from the theatre in the Generalife gardens.

10

4. *Muslim warriors defending the fortress of Islam. A detail from a tenth-century Mozarabic manuscript*

CHAPTER I

It used to be said that in the Maghrib, which originally comprised the northern part of Morocco and most of northern Algeria, when people saw a fellow Muslim looking sad they would say that he was 'thinking about Granada'. But the history of the Muslims of Spain is far more than that of Granada alone, and spans nearly eight hundred years – longer than the history of most modern states. Centuries before the palaces of the Alhambra were built, the Spanish Muslims had created what is recognized as one of the most brilliant civilizations of the world. They were also in part responsible for preserving much of the philosophy and writings of Greek and Roman writers, which would otherwise have been lost when the rest of Europe was emerging from the Dark Ages.

Nevertheless from the beginning the Christians regarded the Muslims as usurpers, and although there were long periods of quiet along the frontiers there was always a determination to drive them back across the Straits. The *Reconquista* was mostly a matter of the gradual eroding of Muslim-held territories, reaching a climax in the last ten years under Fernando and Isabel in the fifteenth century, and the Muslims' defeat was as much due at that time to their own internal quarrels as to Christian determination and the crusading spirit. Granada ended by being the symbol of Muslim or 'Moorish' wealth and luxury, partly because of the beauty of its setting, partly because of the Alhambra's miraculous survival. Yet Granada was in effect the climax of a civilization, or at least the heir to it. The most magnificent period had been before, but would not perhaps have been so appreciated and understood without the existence of the Alhambra.

The first Muslim army, seven thousand strong, landed in Spain in the spring of 711. By that time the Arab empire already stretched eastwards as far as Samarkand and the plains of the Indus. Its capital was Damascus, and that of its north African province, known as Ifriqiya, was Kairouan.

The invaders were mostly Berber tribesmen, whose territories had been conquered by the Arabs in the previous century. Tariq ibn Ziyad was their commander, and the spot close to where they had landed was named after him, Jabal Tariq, or Gibraltar. Within a few months Roderic, the Visigothic king of Spain, 'the Last of the Goths', had been defeated and

. *The approach to Granada. A sketch by Richard Ford, 1831*

killed, and the Muslims were able to capture Córdoba and Toledo. Tariq's overlord, the governor of Ifriqiya, Musa Ibn Nusayr, now followed with a further army of Arabs, and soon much of the peninsula was overrun. In 715 Musa and Tariq went to Damascus with some of their fabulous plunder. And so Spain, which the Arabs called al-Andalus, was added to their vast realm.

There was resistance in the mountainous north-west of Spain, and in 718 the Muslims were beaten at Covadonga. Nevertheless their advance continued across the Pyrenees, and it was only checked at Poitiers in 732.

The Visigoths had not been popular with the indigenous Spanish, who therefore to some extent welcomed their new rulers, especially since the Christian religion and local customs were tolerated. Jews had also been harshly treated by the Visigoths, and it is thought that they abetted the invasion. Soon, however, the Christians found that they had to pay a head-tax, and as a result many decided to become Muslims, thus forming a special class known as Renegados.

Berber Muslims had mostly settled in the cooler north. They began to quarrel among themselves and were discontented. So in 741 more Arabs, from Syria, arrived to quell a civil war, and they too settled in al-Andalus, along the River Guadalquivir. As the original Arabs were Yemenites, this produced yet more conflict. Indeed by this time the whole Arab empire was in a turmoil. In 750 rebels advanced on Damascus, and the caliph's family, the Umayyads, was massacred. Baghdad now became the capital. Only a few Umayyads escaped, and one of them, Abd al-Rahman, whose mother was a Berber, reached al-Andalus in 755. Within a year the various warring parties had accepted him as their head, and he was proclaimed emir of an independent state.

Abd al-Rahman reigned for over thirty years. Although it was an unsettled and bloody period, the country increased in prosperity. In 785 he began to build the famous mosque at Córdoba, which was to rival all others in its splendour. He acquired slaves from across the Pyrenees who were trained as soldiers and then freed. These were known as Slavs, adding another element to the already heterogeneous population.

6. *The interior of the famous mosque at Córdoba, begun by Abd al-Rahman in 785*

7. *The mosaic dome of the Mihrab,*
or prayer recess, in the mosque
at Córdoba

Meanwhile the small Christian kingdoms in the north strengthened their boundaries. Charlemagne, King of the Franks, made an attempt to seize the Muslim outpost of Zaragoza, but had to withdraw, and his defeat at Roncesvalles was to inspire the epic poem *La Chanson de Roland*. There were rebellions by Renegados and others, during succeeding Umayyad emirates, and some were crushed with extreme brutality. In 818 several thousand refugees fled across the Straits to the newly built Fez, which still has its 'Andalusian side'. Real unity was only achieved at the accession in 912 of Abd al-Rahman III, the Victorious, a brilliant statesman. Twenty years later he proclaimed himself caliph. By this time Córdoba had several universities, and was the rival of Baghdad in luxury, with a population of possibly one million.

The power of Abd al-Rahman III extended to northern Africa. He halted Christian raids from the north and created a substantial fleet. A vast and magnificent palace-city, the Medina Azahara, named after the caliph's favourite wife, was built outside Córdoba. Ten thousand men are supposed to have worked at it for twenty-five years, and four thousand three hundred pillars were brought from the ruins of Carthage and elsewhere. Marbles and jaspers were used, doorways in particular were elaborately decorated, and there were gardens, fountains, baths and a pool of quicksilver to reflect the sunset. The palace also had its own mosque and school of learning, as well as accommodation for a garrison of twelve

15

hundred and a harem of six thousand three hundred. By the time of the accession of his son Hakim, Córdoba had reached its zenith of glory, and Muslim military power was at its strongest. Irrigation had transformed agriculture in the south of al-Andalus, and in the mountains there was considerable mineral wealth. Córdoba also became renowned for its craftsmen's skill in textiles, ceramics, leather, metals and glass. Women had a favoured position. Scholars and poets arrived from Baghdad, and there was intense interest in law and religious sciences. Important books of biography and history were written, and Hakim himself is said to have owned a library of four hundred thousand volumes. One reads of orchestras of a hundred lutes and flutes. The oboe, the dulcimer, the psaltery and an early form of the rebec were introduced from the East – as were arabic numerals, the decimal system and in due course the astrolabe.

There was also a toleration of Jewish scholars, physicians and artisans. Young Christians under Muslim rule were said to be fascinated by the Arabic language and learning. It would seem therefore that this great flowering, and the development of what became known as Moorish architecture and artefacts must at least have partly been due to the mingling of races, which included intermarriage. Under Hakim the mosque of Córdoba was doubled in size, and its incomparable Mihrab or prayer-recess was built, with its gorgeous marbles and mosaics, as rich as Kashan rugs. The horseshoe arch was also introduced, originally used in Visigothic architecture. The tower of the mosque, which had been built by Abd al-Rahman III, was considered one of the wonders of the world, and eventually became the model for many others. Other features such as intersecting arches on domes had an influence on Italian Renaissance architecture.

Hakim's son Hisham was only eleven when he succeeded to the caliphate in 976. The new chamberlain, ruthless and an arch intriguer, soon took power. Because of his many brilliant military exploits, he came to be known as al-Mansur (the Conqueror) and to the Christians as the dreaded Almansor. In 997 he sacked the holy shrine of Santiago de Compostela, regarded as the symbol of Christian resistance and by then already a place of pilgrimage, and made his captives carry the bells and gates of Santiago on their backs on the four hundred mile journey to Córdoba. He created his own palace, rivalling the Medina Azahara, and with the labour of his Christian prisoners completed the great mosque, where the bells of Santiago were made into lamps. When Almansor died, two sons in turn succeeded him as chamberlain, the last of them dying mysteriously in 1008. Now, one after the other, the provincial cities revolted. The Berbers destroyed Azahara, and for centuries thereafter it was only a memory, a byword for luxury and grandeur, the only tangible reminders of its glory being some mounds of rubble. In due course a council of ministers in Córdoba abolished the caliphate of the Umayyads. The rapid collapse of this great state, once the wealthiest and strongest in the West, still seems astonishing, almost inexplicable.

At least thirty towns now had virtually their own independent rulers, known as the kings of the *taifas*, often warring against one another. In Ifriqiya there was also, for the time being, a similar collapse of central authority. The richest of these new city-states in al-Andalus was Seville, ruled by an Arab faction. Granada was also powerful, but was under the Zirids, who were Berbers. This period of confusion was of course a splendid opportunity for the Christian kings, in particular Alfonso VI of León, who regarded himself as the heir of the Visigoths. In 1085, after an appeal from the Jewish inhabitants of Toledo whose wealth was about to be confiscated, he entered and captured the city, the original Visigothic capital. It was a great and symbolic moment in Spanish history.

At one stage the Christians had had to pay tribute to the caliphate. Now they were able to exact it from some of the *taifas*. The mighty warrior known as the Cid, forever after one of the national heroes of Spain, went

8. *The Cid, the legendary Spanish hero who fought for both Muslims and Christians during the Reconquest. Here he wields his famous sword, La Tizona*

to Seville to collect some of this tribute and on the way routed the rival forces of the Berber king of Granada. Once regarded as mythical, because of the many legends and ballads around his name, the Cid was in reality a powerful mercenary, now fighting for the Christians, now for the Muslims. After quarrelling with Alfonso VI, he ended as ruler of the Muslim towns of Valencia and Murcia.

In such a century of instability it seems almost anomalous that this should be the golden age of Andalusian poetry, but in some ways the intellectual atmosphere of the *taifas* can be compared to the flowering of the Italian city-states in later centuries. The poetry tended to be extravagant, with an emphasis on love and pleasure, the beauties of nature and the caprices and physical charms of women, and from this there may be a link with the songs of the medieval troubadours. A new poetic form, the *muwashshah*, was invented. The most outstanding poet of all was Ibn Zaydun of Córdoba, who poured out in verse his unhappy love for a Umayyad princess. Another important poet was the last *taifa* king of Seville, al-Mutamid. Schools of astronomy and mathematics appeared in various cities. Literary criticism and debates also flourished. The great writer of the eleventh century in Spain was Ibn Hazam, the grandson of a Renegado, a jurist and a severe theologian, with a sharp tongue, author of a work on the religions of mankind but also of a celebration of chivalric love including verses of his own.

9. *Alfonso VI of León, heir of the Visigoths. This portrait is on his tomb in the cathedral of Santiago de Compostela, Coruña*

10. *Moorish warriors of different tribes, from an eleventh-century manuscript*

Across the sea to the south a vast empire had been built up by fanatic Berbers of nomadic origin, the Almoravids, with their capital at Marrakesh, which they founded. It was the Almoravid king, Yusuf, to whom the poet-king of Seville now appealed for help – realizing that the capture of Toledo by the Christians endangered the whole of the valley of the Guadalquivir, including Córdoba and Seville. Al-Mutamid was aware of the danger to his own position of unleashing this barbarian in Spain but, as he gloomily said, he preferred to be a camel-driver in Africa than a swineherd in Castile. Yusuf duly landed with his Berbers and negroes and defeated Alfonso VI near Badajoz. The muezzin was called from a heap of Christian heads, and afterwards the heads were put in carts and sent to various cities in Spain. This grisly practice of cutting off heads and putting them on display soon spread into the Christian camp.

Tempted no doubt by the luxury he had encountered, but also encouraged by Muslim jurists of the Malikite persuasion (believing in a literal rather than an allegorical interpretation of the Koran) Yusuf decided to return in order to unify the country by annexing the petty *taifas*, at the same time restoring it to the strict precepts of Islam. In 1090 he occupied Granada without a fight, and in the next year Córdoba, and finally, after a long siege, Seville. Al-Mutamid was captured and duly sent to Morocco, and there in miserable conditions he was left to bemoan his fate in poetry.

Yusuf was, however, beaten back by the Cid in various skirmishes. The Cid died in Valencia in 1099, and it is said won his last battle when his corpse was put in armour on his horse and sent out against the enemy. The Muslim city of Valencia only fell to Yusuf after the Cid's wife had burnt it.

Even if the Cid had been fighting for the Muslims, at least he had shown the Christians that the fanatical Almoravids were not invincible. The Almoravids, however, soon became unpopular with their new subjects, particularly the aristocracy. Their soldiers were arrogant and greedy, and the reliance on the Malikite jurists was resented. Rebellions broke out, and there was once again confusion, with a break-up into small states. But the period of Almoravid rule had at least given the Muslims of Spain a stronger sense of the distinctive nature of their religion; while the Christians, goaded by the Church (which offered indulgences for fighting against the Muslims) and the Cluniac monks, were becoming conscious of the ideals of a crusade. Such a *Reconquista* would obviously have to mean the eventual alliance of rival kingdoms.

Now a new Berber dynasty had appeared in North Africa, the Almohads, inspired by a prophet of their own who claimed to be the Mahdi, or divine leader. They swept away the Almoravids and in 1147 captured Marrakesh, and soon their empire extended to Tripoli. Next they turned their attention to a Holy War in Spain, and in 1172 drove out the Almoravids from Seville. The Christians saw themselves faced with a new and more serious threat, and this resulted in the formation of the religious-military Orders of Calatrava and Santiago, which collaborated with the Templars and Hospitallers in defence of sacred territory. Other Orders were formed, and soon they began undertaking punitive expeditions against the Muslims.

In 1195 the Almohads won an important victory against Alfonso VIII of Castile at Alarcos, where twenty-five thousand Spaniards were supposed to have been killed or wounded. Alarm spread through Christendom. The Pope preached a special crusade. Richard Cœur de Lion and Philip II of France considered a joint expedition against the Almohads. In July 1212 the combined forces of Castile, León, Aragon and Navarre, with the aid

11. *The Giralda in Seville, a supreme example of Almohad architecture. A drawing by J. F. Lewis (1805–76)*

12. *A Christian king with his knights. A detail from a thirteenth-century fresco of the conquest of Mallorca*

of the Archbishop of Toledo and knights from across the Pyrenees, won a shattering victory at Las Navas de Tolosa near Toledo. A contemporary chronicler claimed that sixty thousand Muslims had been killed, and the captured silken banner of the Muslims still hangs in the monastery of Las Huelgas in Burgos. It was in effect the end of Almohad power, already weakened by internal quarrels, though this did not become evident until the last caliph died without a son. Now the outstanding Christian leader was Fernando III of Castile, after 1230 also king of León. In a series of brilliant campaigns, Fernando – who was later canonized – captured first Córdoba, then Murcia, and finally Seville in 1248. Muslim rule in Spain was reduced to the sultanate of Granada, largely mountainous but containing the fertile valley of the Vega, as well as Gibraltar and the cities of Ronda, Málaga and Almería. This little sultanate was also to preserve the last embers of Muslim art and learning in Spain.

Even under the 'barbarian' Almohads, scholarship had continued to flourish. The twelfth century was the great age of philosophers in al-Andalus, beginning in effect with Avempace, the Latinized name for Ibn Bajja, who died in 1138. Abubacer, or Ibn Tufail, was born at Guadix near Granada, and became vizier and physician to the caliph at Seville. He was succeeded as court physician by the Cordoban Averroes, or Ibn Rushd, regarded as one of the major philosophers of the world and whose most important work was his commentaries on Aristotle, which was translated into both Latin and Hebrew. Maimonides, or Moses ben-Maimon, the Jewish philosopher and rabbi, another towering intellect, was also from Córdoba. He wrote in Arabic, and his works were translated into Hebrew. In 1160 he had to move to Fez because of persecution, and in due course went to the Levant, becoming physician to Saladin's family. Avenzoar, or Ibn Zohar, born in Seville, was probably the greatest of the western Muslim physicians; he was the first, for example, to attempt a hysterectomy.

Among the other outstanding thinkers of the period were Abenezra, or Moses ben-Ezra, a Jew born in Toledo, author of a major commentary on the Old Testament and an astronomer (a star being named after him); Ibn Jubair of Valencia, poet and author of a travel diary of a pilgrimage to Mecca; Ibn al-Arabi, born in Murcia, a Sufist and great visionary; Ibn Sabin, also of Murcia, who corresponded with the Emperor Frederick II on philosophical matters. A type of vernacular poetry also appeared, known as the *zejel*, associated in particular with Ibn Quzman, who perfected it. Later *zejel* poems were collected in an Egyptian anthology and eventually came to be known as 'Songs of Granada'. Although many theoretical books on music were written, such as Maimonides', there appears to be no precise evidence of what kind of music was played in al-Andalus. The Jews had their own music, and also imitated the *muwashshah* and the romantic songs of the Muslims – examples have been found in an old synagogue in Cairo. As in the previous century there were also numerous works on mathematics, medicine, alchemy and astronomy.

The Muslims of Spain thus provided an intellectual span between East and West. Scholars have noted the influence on Dante, particularly of Ibn al-Arabi. The Benedictine monk Gerbert d'Aurillac, who became Pope Silvester II, read Arabic books when he was at Zaragoza, and revived the liberal arts curriculum of the *trivium* and *quadrivium* which had been followed at Córdoba. Gerard of Cremona made a vast number of translations from Arabic literature; he originally went to Toledo to read Ptolemy's *Almagest*, until then not available in Latin.

As for architecture, in the north of Spain there are a number of 'Mozarabic' examples of the ninth and tenth centuries, the work of Christian refugees from al-Andalus. Of the period of the *taifa* kings two buildings are usually singled out: the mosque in the Aljaferia castle at Zaragoza and the baths at Palma in Majorca. A number of the fortifications of the great castles also date from the *taifas*, as at Almería, Jaén, Ronda, Málaga and Córdoba. The puritanical Almohads in North Africa tended to plaster over elaborate architectural decorations, but in Spain they appeared to allow native craftsmen to develop their aptitude for geometric and floral designs. The supreme example of Almohad architecture is the Giralda tower of Seville, once a minaret and now the belfry of the cathedral. This was begun in stone in 1184 and finished in patterned brickwork with balconies and pointed windows fourteen years later. The same architect is said to have built the rather more simply designed Koutoubia in Marrakesh and the (unfinished) Hassan tower in Rabat.

The Alcázar of Seville is on a Roman site and was probably begun in the eleventh century. It was enlarged by the Almohads, but most of its famous buildings and decorations were later work, by Mudéjares, Muslims under Christian rule. The twelve-sided Golden Tower of Seville, on the banks of the River Guadalquivir, was built in 1220, when the Christian threat to the city became imminent. There is a tradition that Fernando III of León and Castile threatened the Muslim population of Seville with annihilation if a single brick of the Giralda were destroyed. There is also a tradition that the first Christian to climb the Giralda was a Scotsman, Laurence Poore.

13. *A dramatic view of the Alcazaba and the Tower of the Siete Suelos.*
A gouache by Richard Ford from a sketch made in 1831

CHAPTER II

The founder of the Nasrid dynasty that was to rule the sultanate of Granada for nearly two hundred and sixty years, until the Muslims were finally expelled from Spain, was Muhammed Ibn Yusuf Ibn Nasr, also known as Ibn al-Ahmar, but remembered in history as Muhammed I. Described by contemporaries as brave, unpretentious and devoted to his family, he was of noble Arab stock and descended from a companion of the Prophet. In 1227 a fierce and powerful general named Ibn Hud had swept through the Almohad kingdom, beheading, maiming and slaughtering. The future Muhammed I had led a rebellion against him, occupying several important towns, including Jaén. The death of Ibn Hud by poison in 1238 accelerated the disintegration of the old al-Andalus, and it also confirmed the power of his rival, who had ousted him from Granada the year before and was to capture Málaga and Almería. Jaén was soon retaken by the Christians, whose attacks continued under Fernando III. Muhammed now prudently decided to consolidate his domains and became Fernando's vassal, paying an annual tribute and even, in theory, sending representatives to the Cortes, the Castilian equivalent of Parliament. He was also forced to send troops against his fellow Muslims at the siege of Seville.

The sultanate of Granada had about two hundred and fifty miles of coastline, some luxuriant, some craggy, some covered with cicada-haunted cork forest or with prickly pears, some desert with salt-marshes where there were flamingos. The interior, at the most seventy miles deep, had several large mountain ranges, notably the Sierra Nevada and the Serranía de Ronda, with gorges, river beds foaming in winter, mostly dry in summer, and spectacular and savage landscapes, the colour of rust and bruises as V. S. Pritchett has said. But it also contained the rich valley of the Vega, which had been irrigated and intensely cultivated, producing grain, fruit, almonds and sugar. Granada, whose symbol is the pomegranate, was to become famous for its silk, and traders came to buy its gold, silver, lead, iron and sapphires.

Refugees poured into the sultanate. Nearly all the Muslim population of Seville had fled from that city, which was soon a favourite residence for

Don Affonso de Castela ve Toledo ve Leon ... Rey: i ven tes o Compostela ... ta o Reyno D aragon ... e Cordoua, ve Jahen ... ve Seuilla o unrossy ... i ve O urca u gran h

Esta e a primeira cantiga ve loor ve i santa maria ementando os · vii · gojos que oune ve seu fillo. ——

15. *Alfonso X, nicknamed 'the Wise', whose reign was noted for the brilliance of his literary court*

the kings of Castile. Granada stood at the head of the Vega, at the confluence of two rivers, the Genil and the Darro (where gold was found), and beneath the Sierra Nevada, eleven thousand feet high and usually capped with snow. This superbly defensive spot and the beauty of its setting had been recognized by the Muslims since their arrival in the eighth century. Now Muhammed decided to move his seat of government in Granada from the hill of the Albaicín, rising above the rest of the city, to the wooded and cooler heights of the Sabika Hill where there was already a fort, the al-Hambra or Red Citadel. It had two massive protective towers, which still stand today, known as the Torres Bermeyas (the Vermilion Towers), originally erected perhaps by Jewish settlers. He rebuilt this fort, the Alcazaba, adding towers to it, and also erected the

14. *Muslim soldiers going to war.*
   A detail from a fresco showing the conquest of Mallorca, 1229

huge gateway known as the Puerta de las Armas (the Gate of the Weapons). Throughout his domains other castles, large and small, were built or reconstructed, often on sheer promontories or cliffs, and scores of watchtowers and forts were put up along the Mediterranean shore, many again still visible.

Fernando III died in 1252 and was succeeded by Alfonso X, *el Sabio* (the Wise), renowned for his laws and interest in astronomy, and for his lyrics, the *Cantigas de Santa María*. The power of the Castilian nobles was, however, allowed to grow, and Muhammed broke his treaty of vassalage, which had always been resented by the jurists and intellectuals of Granada, and this resulted in fresh battles with the Christians. On Muhammed's death in 1273 his son, Muhammed II, decided to seek help from what is now Morocco, where yet another fanatical and imperialistic dynasty had appeared, the Beni Marin or Marinids. From now onwards the sultans of Granada found themselves involved in some difficult and at times dangerous political manoeuvres, occasionally forcing them to show at least some pretence of honouring treaties of vassalage to the Christians. A notorious incident took place in 1292, when the Marinids crossed the Straits to besiege Tarifa, which had recently been captured by the Christians. The King of Castile's brother, Don Juan, had turned traitor and supported the invaders. He brought his page, the son of the defender of the town, Guzmán, *el Bueno*, and threatened to kill him if Tarifa were not surrendered. Guzmán merely tossed him a dagger from the battlements and withdrew. The boy's throat was thereupon cut.

Brutal episodes such as this spatter the romanticized, often dramatic, but not always glorious story of the next two centuries. As the Spaniards gradually engulfed the sultanate, there were rebellions and court intrigues on both sides. In Granada, sons plotted against fathers and brothers against brothers (nearly all of them bearing the name Muhammed or Yusuf), and on occasions two rival sultans reigned simultaneously. On the other hand, several of the leaders, again on both sides, were men of outstanding taste and intellect. This period saw the creation of the Alhambra and the cathedrals of Toledo and Seville, as well as the transformation by the Spanish kings of the Alcázar of Seville into its present Mudéjar form.

Muhammed II and Muhammed III were both learned and literary men. It was during the reign of the latter that the Alhambra began to take on the character of a palatine or fortress-city, capable of containing forty thousand people; very probably parts of the Generalife – which would have involved the diversion of waters coming from the Sierra Nevada – and the Partal palace within the Alhambra itself belong to this period.

Christian habits and dress were also affected by the people of Granada, and this caused some complaints from fellow Muslims. Only doctors wore turbans, and the sultans would sign documents in the Spanish fashion as 'Don Muhammed'. By the next century, however, the Granadinos seem to have reverted more to the original Arab traditions.

After various revolts by local governors Muhammed III was ousted by his brother Nasr, and his vizier or prime minister was murdered; later he died in prison, poisoned. Nasr was interested in mathematics and astronomy. During his five year reign he managed to beat back King Jaime of Aragon who had besieged Almería, but the Castilians seized Gibraltar. In 1314 he was overthrown by his nephew Ismail I.

Ismail was a warlike and energetic character. He reorganized the army, adding to it a number of Moroccans sent over by the Marinids. The defeat of the Christian army at Elvira, where two Castilian royal princes and a 'lord of Ilketerrah' (England) died, was regarded as a great victory. The body of Prince Pedro was disembowelled, stuffed and displayed on one of

6. *A drawing by David Roberts (1796–1864) of the south façade of the Court of the Alberca, later known as the Court of the Myrtles, and showing the tower of the church of Santa María*

17. *The horseshoe arch leading into the Cuarto Dorado*

Granada's gates. In commemoration of this battle Ismail restored part of the Generalife, as an inscription there relates. He also built the slightly mysterious and dark Mexuar or council chamber of the Alhambra, now the first main room that a visitor enters. Ismail was stabbed to death by his cousin, the governor of Algeciras, for snatching away a particularly beautiful Christian captive. Ismail's son, Muhammed IV, succeeded him, aged about nine. His reign was a turbulent one, with Marinid interventions, Christian encroachments and various internal revolts, but also notable for the appearance of the Renegado Reduán, who became his vizier and whose courtly qualities were to be glorified later in Castilian ballads. Muhammed regained Gibraltar, and went personally to Fez to obtain help from the Marinids. On his return in 1333 he was ambushed and killed, at the instigation of his erstwhile hosts.

Then began the period of greatest splendour for Granada. Muhammed IV was succeeded by his brother Yusuf I, described as reserved and cautious, also as very handsome, large-eyed, elegantly dressed, extraordinarily intelligent, a lover of the arts, interested in mechanical things, with an ability to foresee the future. It was he who, with Reduán still for a while as vizier, created the magnificent Hall of the Ambassadors, which was his audience chamber and throne room, under the Tower of Comares, reflected now so peacefully in the blue-green waters of the

Court of the Myrtles. Yusuf also added the decorations to the Tower of the Captive, and the horseshoe-arched Gate of Justice dates from his reign. In Granada itself he built the Madrasa or university, which became an important centre of learning and a focus for scholars and writers in the western Muslim world. The great days of Córdoba's glory seemed to have been revived.

Yusuf was negotiating peace treaties with Castile and Aragon when the Marinids launched an invasion across the Straits. The son of the Marinid sultan, Abu-l-Hasan, devastated the country around Jerez, but was defeated and killed by the army of Alfonso XI of Castile. Enraged by this news, Abu-l-Hasan in 1340 personally led a new invasion, proclaiming a holy war against the Christians. Yusuf of Granada was constrained to assist his fellow Muslims, and Alfonso XI in his turn declared a crusade, which was joined by Aragon and Portugal, with the Pope's backing. On 30 October a great battle was fought by the River Salado, and the Muslims were decisively routed. The Castilians destroyed Abu-l-Hasan's encampment and slashed down everybody they encountered, including his two wives. He himself only just escaped with his life.

18. *The Comares tower reflected in the waters of the Court of the Myrtles*

The battle of Salado once and for all put an end to major invasions from Morocco. Alfonso XI pressed on with his attacks against the sultanate of Granada, and in 1344 Algeciras surrendered after a long siege. He tried to take Gibraltar, but in 1350 died from the Black Death. In that age of sudden outbursts of chivalry, alternating with hideous cruelty, the Muslims allowed his body to be carried through their lines, and many of their officers wore black mourning bands. A ten-year truce followed.

Alfonso had had help from potentates such as the Duke of Genoa as well as from mercenaries across the Pyrenees. For a while the Earls of Derby and Salisbury had been at the siege. However, the terms of the truce were not considered very honourable for the Christians, and in any case the English had finally been forbidden by Edward III to fight as mercenaries. In Chaucer's *The Knight's Tale* we read:

> *In Gernade* [Granada] *at the seege eek hadde he be*
> *Of Algezir, and riden in Belmarye* [Beni Marin Morocco]

19. *The Court of the Lions, built by Mohammed V in the fourteenth century. A drawing by Harriet Ford (1806–36)*

The object of those lines was to show that the knight was nothing less than an unscrupulous mercenary, ready to sell his services to Christians and Muslims alike. For, odd as it might now seem, there were many Christians fighting as mercenaries for Muslims, and vice versa.

On 19 October 1354 Yusuf I, whilst at prayers in his mosque, was leapt upon by a madman and stabbed to death. He was succeeded by his eldest son, Muhammed V, the eighth Nasrid sultan, also a lover of art and literature. It was Muhammed V who completed the Comares 'quarter' or palace, the official place of government, with its fretted façade supported by columns rising like asphodel stalks, and added another palace for his private pleasure, the Palace of the Lions. Reduán remained vizier. Another of Muhammed V's ministers was Ibn al-Khatib, outstanding among all writers under the Nasrids and astonishingly prolific as an historian, essayist, poet and author of love lyrics. The young poet Ibn Zamrak also worked under him.

After five peaceful and prosperous years court intrigues flared up. Muhammed narrowly escaped from the Alhambra, but Reduán was assassinated, and Ismail II, Muhammed's brother, was proclaimed sultan. Within a year Ismail and another brother were murdered, and the leader of the rebels, a cousin, became Muhammed VI, known in history as *el Rey Bermeyo*, (the Vermilion King). Meanwhile Muhammed V, accompanied by al-Khatib and Ibn Zamrak, had gone to Fez in the forlorn hope of help, and then on to Pedro I of Castile, 'the Cruel'. Muhammed V mobilized his forces at Ronda, and the Vermilion King was forced to flee from Granada, foolishly placing himself at the mercy of Pedro the Cruel, who merely confiscated all his belongings, put him on a donkey and then killed him with his own hands. Muhammed V, once more sultan, was rewarded with the head of his cousin.

There was peace in the sultanate for the last thirty years of Muhammed's life, but war and civil strife were rampant among the Christian states. Pedro in his turn was murdered (in desperate single combat) by his bastard brother, Enrique of Trastamara, who succeeded him. Muhammed was able in the meantime to continue with the embellishment of Granada. He built the Maristán, whose two marble lions were later removed to the Partal in the Alhambra. In his father's Palace of Comares he added the beautiful Sala de la Barca, as an ante-chamber to the throne room, with its many poetic inscriptions and two wooden half-domes with designs like stars. Now – as presumably then – his Palace of the Lions is a dramatic contrast in style, its cloistered arcades showing a decidedly Christian or Roman influence, reminiscent of the peristyles in Pompeian houses, though its profusion of marble columns

33

20. *Moors playing chess. This is thought to be an illustration from an Arabic book on chess and other board games which was translated by Alfonso the Wise for use in his court*

with exotically floral capitals would also seem to have something to do with palm groves. The famous Hall of the Abencerrajes, with its stalactite ceiling, by contrast like icicles, was Muhammed's winter dining-room, while the perfectly proportioned Hall of the Two Sisters was a dwelling-place on two levels, for summer and winter, and where recesses for beds lined with *azulejos* can still be seen. The even more famous fountain, with its twelve heraldic-looking lions, is thought by some to have been brought from a palace down in Granada that belonged to an eleventh-century Jewish vizier.

'There is no conqueror but God.' These words appear again and again in Cufic characters on a background of foliage, as part of the decorations of the Alhambra walls. Other inscriptions appear, in what must seem fantastic profusion to those who can understand Arabic, quoting from the Koran, eulogising in verse the might and achievements of Muhammed V and, occasionally, of his father. These last are in cursive script and consist almost entirely of poems, some of them long and nearly all by Ibn Zamrak, with an endearing self-congratulatory tone. One of the best known is in the Mirador of Lindaraxa, beginning, 'I am a garden adorned with beauty. Gaze upon my loveliness and you will know this to be true.' Another is in the Sala de la Barca, 'I am like a bride in her wedding dress, decorated with every beauty and perfection. Look at this fountain of water and you will understand the abundance of truth which my words contain.' Other poems refer to topical events, such as the circumcision of Muhammed's son in the Hall of the Two Sisters.

The decline and eventual ruin of the sultanate was primarily due to internal feuding, but Arab historians also blame the decadence and luxurious living of the period. Al-Khatib described Granada's great wealth, reflected in the expensive country houses and attire of the women, who were also noted for their beauty, charm and wit: 'rubies, topazes and emeralds gleam from their dresses . . . they are gracious, elegant and slim . . . their breath is like the scent of flowers.' Another writer, though, was less complimentary about all this finery, and described the Granadinas as 'over-blown'. There were times indeed, al-Khatib said, when such heights of luxury bordered on the absurd. The inhabitants of Granada however, paid their taxes and were good Muslims – for by this time there were virtually no Christians left in the sultanate. The city would have abounded in minarets and sparkled with gaily polychrome tiles on roofs and walls. There was also, it would seem, a great love of music.

At the end of his life Muhammed became paranoid and a recluse. Al-Khatib, in terror for his safety, fled to Fez, where he was duly imprisoned

21. *An example of the plaster work on the Alhambra walls – 'a fantastic profusion of Arabic inscriptions'*

22. *The elaborate arched window of the mirador overlooking the Lindaraxa garden*

for 'heresy' and eventually strangled when a mob broke into his prison. His place as vizier in Granada was taken by Ibn Zamrak.

Muhammed died in 1391 and was succeeded by his son Yusuf II, who threw Ibn Zamrak into prison but later recalled him, having first ordered the interim vizier to be beheaded. Within two years Yusuf was dead, poisoned by a ceremonial robe sent to him as a present by the Marinid sultan in Fez.

The next sultan was the bellicose Muhammed VII, who usurped the throne and imprisoned his elder brother, another Yusuf, the rightful heir. Then he had Ibn Zamrak murdered, whilst reading the Koran in his own home; Ibn Zamrak's sons were also stabbed to death, in case of attempts at revenge. Muhammed VII made treaties with the Marinids and Castile but soon broke them. In 1407 he attacked Jaén and Baeza, episodes which inspired the first of the beautiful Castilian ballads which have immortalized the fifteenth-century *Reconquista* in Spanish literature. However, the Muslims lost the important border town of Zahara, west of Ronda. Muhammed decided to have his brother executed, but there is a romantic tale about how Yusuf was saved, partly thanks to the Renegado Mofarrich, but mainly through his being able to prolong a game of chess with his gaoler. In the event the ailing Muhammed VII suddenly died and Yusuf became sultan.

Yusuf III made the faithful Mofarrich his vizier. He might have been pacifically minded but his main Christian opponent, the new Regent of Castile, certainly was not. The Castilians launched an attack on Antequera. During the siege, which lasted five months and in which gunpowder was used for the first time in Spain, Mofarrich was killed and

23. *An eleventh-century marble ablution tank with a carved animal design*

his head was sent as a trophy to the regent. Antequera finally capitulated in 1410, inspiring another ballad which begins in a manner typical of this age of chivalry, describing how the news of the battle came to the ladies of Granada whilst they were watching a sumptuous tournament.

Gibraltar was also captured, by the Marinids, but they were driven out by Yusuf, who managed to get his own protégé on to the throne at Fez. Yusuf built yet another palace within the Alhambra walls, above the gardens of the Partal, but this has since disappeared. The peculiar paintings on leather, possibly by Christian captives or imported Italians, on the ceiling of the Sala de los Reyes, off the Court of the Lions, may also date from his reign. He died of a stroke in 1417 and was followed by his son, Muhammed VIII, a boy of eight, hence *el Pequeño* (the Little One). The vizier, Ali al-Amin, behaved in such a dictatorial manner that he aroused the ire of military chiefs and the formidable clan of the Abencerrajes, and this cost him his life. *El Pequeño* was imprisoned, and his cousin, known as *el Zurdo* (the Left-Handed), became sultan for a while as Muhammed IX. So began a time of constant quarrels and yet more assassinations in the Nasrid family and the opposing clans of Abencerrajes and Bannigas. Sometimes a reign would last only a matter of months.

Between 1417 and 1464 Muhammed VIII was sultan twice, Muhammed IX four times, Yusuf IV for one year only, Muhammed X – known as *el Cojo* (the Lame) – for two years, Yusuf V twice briefly, Muhammed XI – *el Chiquito* (the Tiny) – once, and Saad twice. As a Castilian writer said, 'the Muslims of Granada change their kings as easily as we do shirts.'

So life in the Alhambra was not all contemplation of views, listening to roundelays and watching harem girls in the baths. Nowadays, one reads about those gruesome atrocities as dispassionately as if they were the Grimms' fairy stories.

Muhammed IX was the father, according to Washington Irving, of the three lovely inhabitants, triplets, though each of diverse character, of the Tower of the Infantas; he was 'as brave as he was blundering, and though left-handed wielded his scimitar to such purpose, that he each time reestablished himself upon his throne by dint of hard fighting'. It was during his reign, after he had successfully arranged for the execution of *el Pequeño*, that the spectacular battle of La Higueruela took place, resulting in a triumph for the Castilians under their dashing constable Alvaro de Luna; a battle which came up to the very walls of Granada – and which is depicted on a huge scale as a fresco at the Escorial, providing a splendid if slightly anachronistic document of the battle orders and armaments of the time.

The period in Castilian history is as confusing to follow as it is in Granada's. The Granadinos tried to obtain help from Tunis and Egypt, and after the fall of Constantinople in 1453 from the Ottoman Turks. All the while the Christians were making forays and causing devastation in the Vega, while insisting on tribute and peace agreements. Gibraltar was captured in 1462 by the Duke of Medina Sidonia. The Left-Handed's end came when his throat was cut by his relative Saad in 1453, over the fountain in the room now known as the Hall of the Abencerrajes, given this name because of the legend of the massacre of the chiefs of this clan on the very same spot.

Enrique IV of Castile, known as *el Impotente*, came to the throne in 1454. His undoing was his preference for commoners to nobility, and his disdain for the trappings of chivalry; he also liked wearing Muslim clothes and having a Muslim bodyguard. He actually led an army of perhaps thirty thousand within sight of Granada, but decided not to attack the city because life was 'too precious' to be squandered. The illegitimacy of his daughter, perhaps sired by his friend and counsellor Beltran de la Cueva, and therefore nicknamed *la Beltraneja*, led to ten years of civil war. In 1468 he was forced to acknowledge his half-sister Isabel as heir. Her marriage in the following year to Fernando of Aragon led to the unification of the two kingdoms and eventually to the final defeat of the Muslims of Granada.

24. *The Battle of La Higueruela, a spectacular victory for the Christians*
    which took them to the very walls of Granada. Here a squadron
    of heavily armed knights advances in formation, followed by crossbow-men

CHAPTER III

The final phase of the *Reconquista* lasted eleven years. Like the Trojan War it has been woven about with legends, and has inspired innumerable poems, plays and novels. If there were plenty of episodes which were horrific and gruesome, it was also a war in which chivalry and courtly principles were paramount. In that pre-Cervantes era Spanish nobles and knights went out in their elaborate armour as though for tournaments, with all the paraphernalia of heraldic banners, gold embossed lances, pennants and embroidered caparisons, vying with one another in prowess of arms and usually having first sworn eternal love to some lady of their heart. As is clear from the *romances fronterizos*, or frontier ballads, there was also a strange idealization of the enemy, a kind of pity perhaps, or awe – especially as the war drew on – for the gradual pinching out of this old decadent kingdom with its fabled riches.

On another level the war can be looked upon as the death-struggle in a clash between antagonistic cultures, the end of the Middle Ages in Spain. It was also to prove a testing ground for future Spanish exploits in Italy, the Low Countries and America. The accession of Isabel of Castile put an end to feudal chaos and was the beginning of absolute rule by the monarch. This extraordinary woman – 'queen of earthly queens' to Shakespeare, 'corner stone of the greatness of Spain' to Bacon – led her army with a sense of divine mission. Her portraits show her to have been plain, unsmiling, full-lipped, sad-eyed, with a northern colouring (she was the great grand-daughter of John of Gaunt). Her religious fervour also meant intolerance, and the Inquisition was established in Castile in 1480 under Torquemada who had been her confessor. Yet she was generous and solicitous about her soldiers, who loved her, and showed great courage and endurance. She also, incidentally, had a superb collection of pictures, several of which are now in the royal chapel of Granada.

Although Castile and Aragon were united by her marriage to Fernando, she reserved the administration of Castile for herself and was in effect the dominant partner. Fernando was more the politician and diplomat. A strong soldierly character, with some Jewish blood in him (though this was kept quiet), he had a fleshy face and was a year younger

25 & 26. *Two relief carvings by Rodrigo Alemán (1489–93) from the choir stalls of Toledo cathedral showing the battle of Alhama and the surrender of Alora, two important stages in the Reconquest*

than his wife. He was also something of a philanderer, which often caused distress to Isabel who had strong views on sexual propriety.

The Sultan of Granada at the time of their marriage was Ali, usually known as Muley Hasan and nearly always described as 'fiery'. In familiar Alhambra style he had overthrown his father Saad (the murderer of Muhammed IX), and his reign had begun as a period of prosperity and military success, so much so that in 1476 he felt bold enough to refuse tribute to the 'Catholic Kings', Fernando and Isabel, scornfully announcing that henceforward the mints of Granada no longer coined gold but steel.

He had as his vizier Ibn Reduán Bannigas of Renegado descent, a fact that led inevitably to palace intrigue since the Bannigas clan was so hated by the Abencerrajes. And here we come to one of the most celebrated stories connected with the last years of the Nasrid sultans. The Abencerrajes supported Fatima, Muley Hasan's wife, who was the mother of Boabdil, the heir. This Fatima, in novels sometimes called Ayesha, was in point of fact the daughter of the ill-fated Muhammed IX and thus the sister, or half-sister, of Washington Irving's three princesses – though evidently she was of different calibre to these three lovesick damsels, with her reputation for forcefulness and prudishness, being known as *La Horra* or the Virtuous. Her husband, to her fury, had become enamoured of a Christian slave, Isabel de Solís, renamed Zoraya or Morning Star, who had been promoted to be his favourite wife, bearing him two sons. As Irving said, the harem of this 'voluptuous abode of Moorish monarchs' thus became the 'scene of inveterate jealousies' which were to lead to 'popular commotions and civil wars' in Granada.

In 1481 Muley Hasan attacked and captured the Christian stronghold of Zahara, west of Ronda. The people of Granada were appalled by such rashness and feared reprisals, which were indeed soon forthcoming. When Muley Hasan heard that there was a plot to replace him with Boabdil, he had the prince and his mother imprisoned, so the story goes, in the Tower of Comares. However, the indefatigable sultana knitted scarves together, so that her son could escape down the steep cliff to the Albaicín in the town below, whence he galloped off to safety in Guadix.

Actually the Christians had already decided on a major effort against Muley Hasan. The loss of Zahara was the pretext for a surprise attack, using scaling ladders, on Alhama, deep inside Muslim territory – a masterly affair since the town was built in a superbly defensive position, above a gorge and beneath a tawny sierra rising to eight thousand feet. The town's inhabitants fought back frantically, raining stones and missiles from the towers and battlements, but a quarter of them were

41

27. *Rare portraits of the young Fernando and Isabel, which appear as a seal on a contemporary document*

slaughtered the first day, including women and children sheltering in the mosque.

This battle, under the command of the Marquis of Cádiz, and succeeding victories in the campaign during the next year are illustrated in interesting contemporary reliefs in the choir of Toledo Cathedral. Cannons, muskets and crossbows are shown in the storming of Alhama. Usually these reliefs depict the Christians as clean-shaven and wearing helmets, whereas the Muslims are bearded and wear turbans, with swords and slings as weapons (in actual fact the Muslims were very well equipped, though inferior in artillery, and were especially skilled in the crossbow and arquebus). Sometimes the Christian foot-soldiers wear leather cuirasses over their chain-mail, making one realize the importance of their greater mobility over the ponderously armoured knights.

Old Muley Hasan now marched out into the Vega and across the wild countryside around Alhama, and proceeded to cut off the town's water supply. The situation for the Christians became desperate, but was saved by the arrival of the Duke of Medina Sidonia, coming to the rescue in spite of his hereditary feud with the Marquis of Cádiz. In Granada the news of the loss of Alhama was regarded as 'an arrow through the heart' and inspired a famous ballad, *¡Ay de mí! Alhama*, to be translated by Byron with the once much quoted refrain 'Woe is me, Alhama!', and also to be turned into a song by the sixteenth-century Granadino poet Luis de Narváez. Fighting within the city broke out, one faction demanding the return of Boabdil. If there is truth in the story (one of many) of Muley Hasan beheading seven leading Abencerrajes in the room that now has their name, perhaps it happened at this moment. At any rate the Abencerrajes brought Boabdil back to Granada, forcing his father to flee and join his brother, Boabdil's uncle, familiarly known as El Zagal (the Valiant). Alhama remained as an isolated city in Christian hands, under the command of the Count of Tendilla.

Boabdil, the name given to him by the Spaniards as a corruption of Abu Abdullah, now became the sultan Muhammed XII, while his father continued to control a large part of the Muslim domains. Like some of his

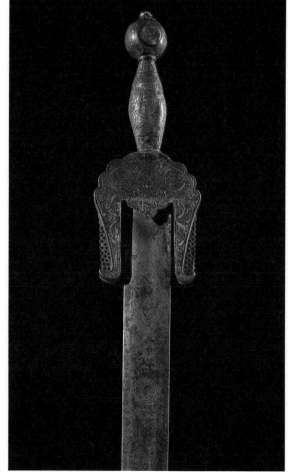

28. *A Muslim sword with a brass hilt, from fourteenth-century Granada*

predecessors he was small – hence the nickname *el Rey Chico* (the Boy King). Aged nineteen or twenty at the time, he is not considered to have been endowed with a strong character, though he was courageous in battle and writers have always regarded him with affection. It was his father who sent a relief force to Loja, not far from Alhama, when it was besieged by King Fernando, even though the town was under the command of Boabdil's father-in-law, Ali Atar, a fine old warrior, and an octogenarian, whose name is still commemorated in a main square of the Albaicín in Granada. It was Muley Hasan too who led a successful attack along the coast near Gibraltar.

Fernando had been anxious to make his personal mark in the war, but now – in the parching heat of July – he allowed himself to be drawn into an ambush by Ali Atar. It was a bad defeat, with many prisoners taken by the Muslims and at least eight hundred Spaniards killed, including the Grand Master of Calatrava. The Marquis of Cádiz managed to escape, but lost two brothers. The 'best blood of Andalusia' was shed, so the chroniclers tell us. Boabdil now bestirred himself and marched out against the town of Lucena, well beyond the frontier and on the road to Córdoba. He was joined by his father-in-law Ali Atar, but the results were fatal. Ali Atar was killed by a lance thrust and his body swept away down the river until caught by some rocks. Boabdil fought well but had been forced to dismount. He was attacked by three soldiers and captured. The Spanish commander, the Count of Cabra, in accordance with the principles of chivalry, spared Boabdil's life and incarcerated him in the citadel of Lucena. The date was 20 April 1483, a turning-point in the war.

Today Ali Atar's sword is displayed in the Army Museum in Madrid, along with Boabdil's, richly enamelled and inlaid with ivory and gold. Boabdil's fine carmine-coloured tunic is also there, embroidered with gold filigree, as well as his white turban adorned with gold, his leather leggings and barbouches. In memory of the battle the escutcheons of the counts of Cabra still show a Moor's head wearing a crown.

Boabdil's mother Fatima sent emissaries to the Catholic Kings with proposals for his release. Eventually a treaty was negotiated: in return for Boabdil's release there would be a two years' truce, the surrender of several prisoners, a large annuity, a free passage for the Christians across the sultanate for carrying on the war against Muley Hasan, and the handing over of Boabdil's son and the sons of his chief nobility as hostages. For the Muslims Boabdil had now earned himself the additional sobriquet of *el Zogoybi* (the Unlucky One).

Meanwhile Muley Hasan had taken the opportunity of returning to the Alhambra, while Fatima installed herself on the Albaicín hill opposite.

29 & 30. *Relief carvings from the choir stalls at Toledo cathedral.The first shows the attempted assassination of the king and queen (see page 51), and the second the surrender of Granada by Boabdil*

She was joined by Boabdil, but the ensuing turmoil in Granada forced him to leave, this time for Almería. During the next three years there were frequent forays by the Christians, causing much devastation of crops, and some important towns were captured, in particular Zahara, Alora, Marbella and Ronda, once thought impregnable. Many Christian prisoners, in a ghastly state, were released from Ronda, their chains being sent for display on church walls throughout Castile.

Isabel, in spite of frequent pregnancies (one child being the future Catherine of Aragon, Henry VIII's queen), was the guiding spirit of the war, more even than her husband, who for a while had been tempted by territorial ambitions in France. In particular she concentrated on improving the artillery and methods of transportation, and she also formed 'queen's hospitals' for the soldiers. The Castilian fleet patrolled the Straits, to discourage landings from Africa.

Volunteers from abroad arrived to take part in this crusade, and there was also a contingent of Swiss mercenaries, with a reputation for toughness and religious zeal. One grand foreigner was an Englishman, the 'Conde de Escales', alias Lord Scales, of the Woodville family and therefore considered royal. Isabel rewarded his presence with some costly gifts, including twelve Andalusian horses and pavilions hung with cloths of gold.

The text within the manuscript illustration reads:

Le viables se fa pencheyne emsim.

Le viable li say adehr mon vana uanetm.

Le viables say ais aymacens sar comm ebolims ecomm per amor re lous ronas.

Le viables say merpar les aymacens per hmons re lous ronas. :.

32. *Scenes of wooing, hawking, jousting and feasting from a fifteenth-century Catalan manuscript. Knightly encounters and chivalrous pursuits were characteristic of the final phases of the Reconquest – a late flowering of Medieval ideals*

Sometimes Fernando and Isabel had to remonstrate with their nobles about their ostentation and gorgeous clothes, equipage and armour – unpleasant to wear, one would have thought, in Andalusian heat. Yet the sovereigns themselves appeared to regard the battlefield as a place for finery. At the siege of Moclín Isabel sat on her chestnut mule in a chair embossed with gold and silver, and with a bridle of satin, while Fernando was dressed in a crimson doublet and yellow satin breeches, with a brocaded mantle over his cuirass. We are told that Lord Scales, who was with them, wore chain-mail with a French surcoat of silk; he also had a

31. *(opposite) This detail from the fresco of the Battle of La Higueruela shows both heavy and light cavalry, and gives an indication of the finery sported by some of the Christian knights in battle*

French hat with plumes, and his horse had caparisons of 'azure silk, lined with violet and sprinkled over with golden stars, that swept the ground'.

There are conflicting stories about the fate of Boabdil's younger brother Yusuf. One is that his own father had him (and other younger sons) put to death for fear of plots, and another is that El Zagal did the deed, and that Muley Hasan went blind with grief. At any rate Fatima was taken prisoner by El Zagal, and Boabdil had to flee from Almería, shamefully taking refuge in Córdoba. Then the people of Granada decided to get rid of the aged Muley Hasan and replace him with his brother, El Zagal. An excellent first impression was made in Granada by the arrival of old El Zagal, who came with several prisoners of the Order of Calatrava and in a cavalcade of seventy horsemen, each with a Christian head dangling from the saddle.

When Muley Hasan died, El Zagal gave him a pauper's burial and, to be on the safe side, according to some, imprisoned Zoraya in the building now known as the Tower of the Captive. He became the Sultan Muhammed XIII.

Not for nothing was Fernando a model for Machiavelli's *The Prince*. He sent Boabdil back to Granada, where some discontent with El Zagal had soon begun to grow. The ruse was successful, and as he had hoped civil war flared up between the rival factions, as usual based on the Albaicín and the Alhambra. Eventually, however, an agreement was reached between uncle and nephew, whereby the sultanate would be divided in two, with El Zagal, as Muhammed XIII, retaining a triangle of territory based on Granada, Málaga and Almería, and with Boabdil, Muhammed XII, ruling the rest. This of course was not at all to Fernando's liking; he accused Boabdil of being unlawfully in league with his uncle, and immediately sent out an army against him at his headquarters at Loja.

The town of Loja was regarded as the key to the Vega. Above were the arid mountains, of volcanic origin, grey and gnarled with the famous gorge of Los Infiernos (literally The Hells) and La Peña de los Enamorados (The Rock of the Lovers), from which a Muslim maiden and a Christian knight are supposed to have hurled themselves locked in each other's arms. Around the town were well-watered lush meadows with their white country houses, which the Granadinos now call *cármenes*, still a feature of the Vega. It was a great prize and the battle lasted thirty-four days – illustrated in one of the reliefs in Toledo Cathedral. Lord Scales's archers played an important part, and the English leader lost three teeth. 'It is little to lose a few teeth,' he told the anxious Queen Isabel, 'in the service of Him who has given us all.' Boabdil was wounded twice and as a result treated with chivalric respect. But Fernando imposed even harsher

48

terms than before: once Boabdil had regained his throne, he would have to give up Granada and retire to the more desolate land around Guadix, now as probably then noted for its cave-dwellers.

Other victories followed for the Christians in 1486, at Illora and Moclín. In the cathedral of Sigüenza in northern Castile there is a superb recumbent monument to a young man in armour reading a book: Martín Vásquez de Arce, known as *El Doncel* (the King's Page) *de Sigüenza*. He was killed in that year, evidently while saving the life of the Duke of Infantado in a mountainous pass to the north of Granada.

The policy of Fernando was to 'pick out the seeds of the pomegranate one by one', so early in 1487 the Catholic Kings decided to concentrate on Málaga.

This wealthy city, embellished by Yusuf I, was the second in the sultanate after Granada, as well as its main port, a 'paradise on earth' to Muslim writers. There were fears too that the Turks might send ships there. First, however, the neighbouring town of Vélez Málaga had to be taken. The siege of this place was notable for the near escape of Fernando, who could not draw his sword from its scabbard whilst in the thick of battle. El Zagal had come hurrying down but was beaten back, and Vélez Málaga surrendered. Meanwhile Boabdil had returned to Granada, having claimed that El Zagal had murdered his father, Muley Hasan. The fickle Granadinos were only half convinced, and had been impressed by El Zagal's brave and immediate response to this new incursion by the Christians. But defeat was a different matter, and El Zagal returned to find the gates of Granada shut against him, and his nephew with his formidable mother installed in the Alhambra.

Málaga was defended by a hardy old chieftain, Hamet al-Zegri, once the governor of Ronda and determined on revenge against the Christians. He had with him a number of Berber mercenaries, known as Gomeres, and several Renegados, who knew that they would be doomed if captured by the Christians. Indeed the siege of Málaga, lasting three and a half months at the height of summer, was one of the bitterest battles in the whole war.

Isabel arrived with a retinue of ladies and cavaliers. The Toledo reliefs give us an idea of the splendour of the encampment with its cone-shaped pavilions, which must have been a beautiful sight indeed against the backdrop of the sea. The Christian army has been estimated at between sixty and ninety thousand men. Isabel took strict control over their welfare and morals, forbidding gambling and swearing, and of course prostitutes. An abundance of priests made sure that the Spaniards remembered the holy nature of the crusade against the infidel.

49

33. *The triumphal entry of the Catholic Kings, with the three Infantas and Cardinal Mendoza, into Granada in 1492. A coloured relief in the Capilla Real in Granada cathedral*

34. *One of the many fortified towns which dot the landscape around Granada. A painting by Soloman Caesar Malan, c. 1830*

We read of constant cannonades, wooden towers on wheels, 'tortoises' of shields, catapults, boiling pitch and the use of mines; of the clash of swords against axes, of arrows from crossbows and volleys from arquebuses. The Aragonese fleet blocked the harbour. El Zagal valiantly sent an army from Almería, but it was routed – to the disgust of many Muslims – by a contingent sent by Boabdil, in accordance with his treaty of vassalage with Fernando. As famine began to increase within the besieged city, a desperate ruse was thought up. A dervish allowed himself to be captured by the Christians, who were impressed by his wild appearance and declamations, and foolishly brought him into their camp. During the time of siesta the man suddenly drew a dagger and leapt upon two grand Spanish personages, in the mistaken belief that they were the king and queen. He was at once slashed down by attendants, and his body was catapulted over the walls into Málaga. In retribution the Gomeres troops killed an important Christian captive, tied him to a donkey and drove the animal towards the enemy.

People were dying in the streets in Málaga, and there were terrible diseases. At last Hamet al-Zegri withdrew with his men into the celebrated citadel of Gibralfaro above the city, while a wealthy merchant negotiated a surrender with the Christians. First, however, the merchant tried threats: all the fifteen hundred prisoners would be killed and their bodies hung from the battlements if his terms were not accepted. To this Fernando replied that if a single Christian were harmed, every man, woman and child within Málaga would die. There was no alternative but unconditional surrender.

The long and stubborn resistance of the Muslims, the great number of Spanish dead, the heavy expense of the campaign and the hot weather did not put Fernando into a lenient mood. He also wanted to make Málaga an example to other towns in the sultanate. As a result virtually all its citizens, having been first tricked into handing over their possessions as part of the ransom, were either deported, sold into slavery, exchanged with Christian prisoners in North Africa or given away as presents. Fifty of the prettiest girls were given to the Queen of Naples, and thirty to the Queen of Portugal. After the surrender of the Gibralfaro citadel, a hundred Gomeres were sent to the Pope, while Hamet al-Zegri was bound with chains and flung into a dungeon. Renegados were tied to stakes and run through with lances by horsemen, and there were *autos de fe*

35. Detail from a fresco showing the defence of Mallorca. The defenders were noted for their use of the sling

for Muslims who had pretended to be converted to Christianity but had stuck to their former faith. The fortunate were four hundred and fifty Jews, who at least escaped with their lives though not without a heavy ransom.

The streets were purified and swept, and the main mosque turned into a cathedral. Then Queen Isabel entered barefoot behind an effigy of the Virgin of Victory.

The whole of the western part of the Nasrid sultanate, to within a few miles from Granada, was now in Christian hands. Most of the eastern territories, as far as the Christian province of Murcia, were under the control of El Zagal, and these included the towns of Almería, Guadix and Baza as well as the mountainous area of the Alpujarras, so rich in minerals and a centre for the manufacture of silk. While El Zagal continued with some success to make local attacks on the Christians, Boabdil remained happily and luxuriously in the Alhambra, even sending congratulations to the Catholic Kings on the capture of Málaga.

In 1488 Fernando succeeded in annexing about a third of El Zagal's land, though not without some fierce retaliation. By May 1489 he was ready for an assault on Baza, which was under the command of El Zagal's brother-in-law, Prince Cidi Yahye. It was to be the costliest and most protracted, and ultimately the most decisive, campaign of the war.

Today in the Alameda (or promenade) of Baza you can still see some of the Christians' iron cannons, bound together with hoops. This Alameda is partly on the site of the old garden district, which Fernando first had to capture. The battle was a gory one, with many casualties on both sides. If it had not been for the enthusiasm and faith of Isabel, whose court had been moved to Jaén to the north, Fernando might well have withdrawn. She worked hard to obtain supplies and have roads improved. She raised funds from the Church and other sources, and pledged her crown and jewels for loans from merchants in Valencia and Barcelona.

The siege was notable for single combats between Christians and Muslim knights, though Fernando discouraged this. Among the Spanish nobles were powerful figures such as the Marquis of Cádiz, the Count of Tendilla, the Count of Cabra, Don Alonso de Aguilar and his brother Gonzalo de Córdoba, the future *Gran Capitán* of legendary fame. Fernando cut down all the prized trees in the gardens, and built palisades and moats encircling Baza. The siege dragged on until late autumn, and there was no sign of surrender. The Christian army was being reduced by sickness, and when a storm nearly swept away its camp the morale of the troops suffered so much that Fernando asked the queen to come from Jaén – such was the charismatic effect of her personality.

She came, and in full state, accompanied by the Cardinal of Spain, Mendoza, with banners and military music, a glittering cavalcade. The priest-historian known as Peter Martyr has said: 'Her presence seemed at once to gladden and reanimate our spirits.' To the people of Baza it was proof that the Christians were ready to continue the siege throughout the winter. When Cidi Yahye emerged for a parley with the Catholic Kings, he was so overwhelmed by Isabel's presence that he secretly agreed to become a Christian. He went to El Zagal at Guadix and persuaded him not only that Baza must be surrendered but that further resistance throughout the old sultan's domain was in vain.

This time the terms for the Muslims, in contrast to the cruelty at Málaga, were generous and mild. El Zagal met the Catholic Kings outside Almería and was entertained to a royal banquet. The great seaport, the Portus Magnus of the Romans, was entered without a fight on 23 December.

El Zagal was given a large sum of money and the tutelage of a coastal area, including some salt-mines, with the title of King of Andaraz. But to be lord of a few salt-mines and a handful of castles was no substitute for a sultanate and dreams of the Court of the Myrtles and the Generalife gardens, and in due course he removed himself and his family to Fez. Here this once valiant warrior found himself execrated as a coward and betrayer. He was arrested, imprisoned and blinded, and all his wealth was confiscated. Later he was turned out and left to wander as a beggar.

The population of Granada had now swollen to some two hundred thousand, including a number of Renegados of Christian origin and perhaps Jews, refugees for political reasons or from the Inquisition. To the outside world this great city was without doubt doomed, as if some fabulous and once proud beast had reached its dying agony. Yet its people became suddenly imbued with an extraordinary energy, a new valour, whether out of desperation, or a false sense of security behind those massive fortifications, or in the hope of help from Africa or the Turks, or simply out of religious fervour, in defence of this last bastion of Spanish Islam, almost seven hundred and fifty years old.

After the defeat of El Zagal it was assumed by the Catholic Kings that the war was over, in accordance with the treaty of Loja. But the mood in Granada made it impossible for Boabdil to comply, or so he maintained, and in any case there had been a time limit to the treaty's conditions. When the Christians began a systematic policy of ravaging and laying waste the Vega, Boabdil himself or his warlike general Musa led some successful attacks against enemy fortresses. The people of Guadix, Baza and Almería also became restless and an uprising was plotted – with fatal

36. *The sultans of Granada as they appear on the ceiling of the Hall of Justice in the Court of the Lions*

results for themselves, since it was suppressed in time by Fernando, and this involved not only the loss of all the privileges originally granted to them but mass deportations to Africa.

Fernando and Isabel spent the winter in Seville carefully preparing for the final attack. On 11 April 1491 their army set out, and by the 26th it was encamped at Ojos de Huescar, almost within view of Granada. The Catholic Kings had sworn never to return until the cross flew from the towers of the Alhambra.

This last campaign more than any other was notable for its series of knightly encounters and individual feats of bravery on both sides, almost as if it were some prolonged tournament, consciously signalling the end of the Middle Ages in Spain. Some of these episodes are fantasy, but true or not nearly all were celebrated in verse and ballads. Among the most daring of the Muslim cavaliers was Tarfa, who went so far as to leap over the Christians' barricades and to plant a lance near the royal tents with a label on it saying that it was for the queen. This insult so shocked the Spaniards that Hernán Pérez del Pulgar, who had already proved himself a superb fighter outside Baza, crept one night into Granada by a secret route and fixed a scroll with the words 'Ave Maria' on the doors of the main mosque.

Isabel would often appear in full armour of burnished steel as she rode on her war-horse about the encampment, solicitous as always about her troops' welfare. On one occasion she decided to move closer to Granada, in order to get a better view of the city, and chose the small village of La Zubia. As usual she was accompanied by a retinue of magnificence, but to be on the safe side the Marquis of Cádiz had brought up some of his men, halberdiers and crossbowmen, though with instructions from the queen not to provoke any bloodshed. The Muslims, however, could not endure this display of bravado and marched out of Granada. When their opponents refused to be drawn into battle, the story goes that the burly Tarfa rode out in front of their lines, in full armour and with his vizor down, and with the scroll inscribed 'Ave Maria' tied to his horse's tail. This piece of sacrilege induced Fernando to allow a young knight, Garcilaso de la Vega, although more slightly built than Tarfa, to challenge him in single combat. The laws of chivalry were strictly observed by the onlookers and neither side intervened. Both men were eventually unhorsed, and at the last minute, just as Garcilaso was about to be stabbed, he ran Tarfa through with his sword. The Muslims could not now contain themselves, and they attacked. A big battle broke out, and they were driven back. Isabel is supposed to have escaped death or capture by hiding in a laurel bush.

37. Auto da fe. *The Inquisition pursued those Muslims who had pretended to be converted, but had in fact retained their faith. A painting by Pedro Berruguete, c. 1490s, court painter to Fernando and Isabel*

Fernando determined to wreck whatever was left of the once rich and beautiful Vega, and this he did right up to Granada's walls. Some chroniclers write of the Muslims standing aghast on the battlements as they watched the smoke and the devastation. Some say that Boabdil, *el Rey Chico*, led what was to be the last sortie, and that he barely escaped, having been unhorsed and wounded. Disaster, however, enveloped the Christians, for in the middle of July Isabel's tent caught alight, the flames sweeping right through the camp, completely destroying it along with a huge amount of precious war material, gorgeous brocades, jewellery, and gold and silver plate. This conflagration is often supposed to have resulted in a royal decision to build Santa Fe, a quadrangular town plainly laid out like a barracks, or a Roman *praesidium*, and it is said that it was created in eighty days. However, there is documentary proof that Santa Fe was begun well before June. The town flourishes today, no great beauty and still with a strong military atmosphere, and one can imagine the place thronged with halberdiers, horses and knights. Over the door of the church are carved a lance and a scroll with the words 'Ave Maria', commemorating the gallantry of Hernán Pérez del Pulgar.

As the threat of famine grew within Granada, and insurrection seemed imminent, Boabdil began secret negotiations for a surrender. There are

38. *A narrow street in the Albaicín*

39. *The Dar-al-Horra last of the Nasrid palaces in the Albaicín*

many conflicting accounts of succeeding events, and some of them are fictional, but again a few original documents survive. The negotiations took place at night, between Fernando's secretary Fernando de Zafra, Boabdil's vizier Abul Cazim, and the constable of the Alhambra, Aben Comiza. Once Fernando de Zafra actually entered the Alhambra with Gonzalo de Córdoba. Finally, after long haggling, on 25 November the terms were agreed. Most important, the inhabitants of Granada were to be allowed to retain their religion, customs, laws and dress, and their property would be respected. Taxes would not be heavier than hitherto, and Christians would be punished if they entered Muslim houses. Prisoners would be exchanged and hostages returned, and safe passage would be granted for anyone wanting to emigrate to Africa. The safety of Boabdil and his family would also be guaranteed, and he was to be granted a small 'kingdom' in the Alpujarras, in vassalage to Fernando and Isabel, with a large sum of money and other benefits.

The actual date of surrender was to be 6 January 1492, but Boabdil was aware that the Granadinos were becoming suspicious and he asked for the

40. *An old photograph of the steep cobbled lanes of the Albaicín*

date to be advanced. On the night of 1 January, hostages having been sent to the Christian camp, he admitted a large armed force into the Alhambra and received the commander, Gutierrez de Cardenas, in his throne room in the Tower of Comares. The keys were handed over, and three cannon shots were fired, signifying that the occupation of the Alhambra was complete.

The Spaniards were ready to advance at first light in full pomp and splendour. The cavalcade was preceded by the Cardinal of Spain, and according to some it was he who entered Granada and raised the silver cross of the crusade and the banner of St James above the Alcazaba's tower, with its sweeping view of the ruined Vega and the distant sierras. Another version is that the Count of Tendilla had already entered the Alhambra, and that the flag was first raised above the Tower of Comares. Traditionally it is also said that Boabdil left the Alhambra through the

Tower of the Siete Suelos (or Seven Floors), which had been used as a prison for Christian knights; the tower's gate was thereupon blocked up, in case of ill omen.

Boabdil met the king and queen outside a small Muslim shrine, or *rabita*, now known as the hermitage of San Sebastián. Again the truth is entangled with romance. Some say the dejected *Rey Chico* kissed the hand of Fernando, or perhaps his sleeve, but the real evidence contradicts this. It seems that the dowager sultana Fatima had strongly opposed such humiliation. At any rate Boabdil was treated with respect and even sympathy, and he was at last reunited with his son, who had been a hostage since the battle of Moclín. A theory is that he actually lingered for weeks in the Albaicín before setting out for exile in the Alpujarras, taking with him the bones of Nasrid ancestors which had been exhumed in the Alhambra. Some half dozen miles from Granada, as he entered the mountains, he looked back in the hope of a last glimpse of his beloved city, and wept. His mother turned on him, and unkindly upbraided him for his tears: 'You do well to weep like a woman for what you could not defend like a man.' This spot is now known as El Ultimo Suspiro del Moro, The Last Sigh of the Moor.

The departure of Boabdil is also celebrated by one of the most famous of the ballads, written in about 1500. It was translated by John Gibson Lockhart as *The Flight from Granada*. The first verse begins:

> *There was crying in Granada when the sun was going down –*
> *Some calling on the Trinity – some calling on Mahoun!*
> *Here passed away the Koran – there the Cross was born –*
> *And here was heard the Christian bell – and there the Moorish horn.*

Fernando and Isabel entered the Alhambra, but retired at once to Santa Fe, in order to make their triumphant entry on 6 January, so that they could first give thanks to the Virgin of Victory in the old mosque turned now into a cathedral. One longs for a first-hand account by a Spaniard on seeing the Alhambra and its sumptuous halls and gardens. (There is, however, an inventory of a fantastic collection of rugs, silks and ceramics, presumably mostly sent on mules and horses to Boabdil in the Alpujarras.) The family of the Count of Tendilla was appointed hereditary governors of the Alhambra.

The taking of Granada was received with immense joy throughout Christendom. A high mass was celebrated in St Peter's, and a special *Te Deum* was sung at St Paul's in London.

CHAPTER IV

The year 1492 was in another sense an *annus mirabilis* for Spain, for it was the year in which Columbus discovered America. After long frustrations and attempts to interest various European governments in the project of reaching Asia from the west, he had eventually turned to Fernando and Isabel. Then in 1491, having at last given up hope, he decided to take his proposals to the King of France. Suddenly, however, there was a dramatic recall to the sovereigns who were at Santa Fe, and Columbus was with them when Granada fell. Much bargaining lay ahead, and Fernando was inclined to withdraw from the negotiations. It was Isabel who became enthusiastic, recognizing the genius beneath the bombast, and once again, as at the battle for Baza, she announced that she was ready to pledge her crown and jewels. The final agreement to sponsor the expedition, comprising three ships and a hundred and twenty men, was reached on 17 April.

But 1492 was also the year of the expulsion of the Jews from Spain, and Fernando and Isabel signed the decree for this on 30 March. Throughout the previous decades – and not only because of the recently founded

41. *The famous Alhambra vase, over four feet high*

42. *The Alcaicería. The old silk market is all that remains of the many markets which used to cluster round the Great Mosque*

Inquisition – the Jews had been suffering violent bouts of persecution. There had been a particularly horrific pogrom in 1391, and in 1473 ghettos had been sacked at Jaén and Córdoba. After 1484 all the Jews had been expelled from Christian-held Andalusia and their property appropriated as a way of paying for the war. Like the Mudéjares (the Muslims who lived in Christian territories), the Jews had in many cases been forced to wear distinctive clothing, badges or hair styles. Those who decided to convert to Christianity were contemptuously called *marranos*, pigs. Absurd rumours had multiplied about the Jews: they drank Christian blood and ritually crucified children. The Inquisition also became an outlet for personal animosities, rivalries and vindictive denunciations. It has been said that in its first ten years seven hundred people were burnt to death, and some thousands 'reconciled' – a polite term – through *autos de fe*. For Isabel, however, this final solution was not just a matter of seizing the Jews' wealth, but through deep religious conviction, intensified after ten years of waging a holy war against unbelievers.

The Jews of the Sephardim, as the Spanish Jews called themselves, had until the end of July to leave. The rules about selling their property were absurd and cruel. Perhaps four hundred thousand people were involved – estimates vary. Some accepted the humiliating alternative of baptism, some fled to Portugal; but the Catholic Kings soon persuaded the Portuguese to expel their Jews also. For sheer misery the stories of the journeys to exile can hardly be surpassed, involving crowded, leaking ships, famine, disease, plague, harassment and murder by brigands. The main destinations were to North Africa, Italy and the Levant. Even today in Turkey there are Sephardic Jews who still speak old Castilian, and their traditional songs can be heard in many places around the Aegean and on the Dalmatian coast.

As for Boabdil, within months he became unhappy in his so-called kingdom in the wilds of the Alpujarras mountains. His chief supporters, the powerful Abencerrajes, soon decided to remove themselves to North Africa. After the death of his wife, Boabdil negotiated the sale of his lands to the Christians, and with some thousands of followers, went to Fez – bravely, one would have thought, after the experience of his uncle, El Zagal. However, he was well treated and built palaces in the Andalusian manner. He is supposed to have died in 1536, aged sixty-three and white-bearded, helping the caliph of Fez to fight against Berber rebels; his body was put in a swift-flowing river so that it could be swept out to sea.

The Catholic Kings sometimes stayed in the Alhambra, and Granada became an important military centre in their subsequent wars in Italy and Africa. They spent much money in repairing and fortifying the Alhambra, making the towers more squat so as to be less vulnerable to artillery fire. Within the buildings the chief relic of their alterations is near the main entrance: the Cuarto Dorado or Golden Room, so called because of the ceiling painted with the then fashionable grotesques. After Isabel died in 1504, Fernando married Germaine de Foix, who had an apartment above the Cuarto Dorado.

The Count of Tendilla took over what had been the palace of Yusuf III near the Partal gardens. The Catholic Kings gave the site of another palace further east within the Alhambra precincts to the Franciscans, who built a monastery there. This palace seems to have been laid out on the lines of the Generalife and would have been of the same period. After their deaths Fernando and Isabel were buried in the monastery, but when the new cathedral was completed in Granada, their bodies were removed to the royal chapel, to lie side by side in simple lead coffins in the crypt, with sumptuous Renaissance tombs on the floor above.

The Albaicín, with its steep cobbled lanes and crowded white houses, and where the minarets with horseshoe windows have been converted into church towers, is full of the atmosphere of its Muslim past. The Church of San Nicolás faces what must be one of the great views of the world – the Alhambra towers with the Sierra Nevada beyond. Near the Church of El Salvador, on the site of the Albaicín's main mosque and incorporating some remains, is one of the last of the Nasrid palaces, that of

Dar al-Horra, built for some princesses in the mid-fifteenth century. Below, in the main town, much rebuilt, there is still a feeling of a *souk* in the Alcaicería, once the silk bazaar. This leads into the Plaza de Bibarrambla, used in Muslim times for jousts and tournaments and by Christians for bullfights and fiestas. Two of the grandest and most interesting of the remaining Muslim houses are the Casa de los Girones and the Cuarto Dorado de San Domingo, where Torquemada also lived.

The Casa de los Tiros is Mudéjar, i.e. built after the Christian conquest. Up in the Albaicín pottery known as *fajalauza* is still made using designs reminiscent of Muslim times. Relatively few objects used to furnish or decorate the Alhambra and other palaces are in the museums, but this on the whole is not surprising since most of the functional furnishings of the palaces would have been composed of rugs, cushions and divans, made of the silk for which Granada was famous. The most outstanding piece of furnishing that remains is the huge and beautiful 'Alhambra Vase', shaped like an amphora – cerulean blue and turquoise with a smoky golden-brown lustre, wing-handled and with designs of gazelles and leaves. The Count of Tendilla is supposed to have found this filled with gold, and it was used with several other similar vases to decorate his descendants' garden. All the other vases have vanished, unless they are those now in

43. *The tomb of Fernando and Isabel in Granada cathedral. A drawing by David Roberts*

museums in Madrid, Leningrad, Stockholm and Palermo.

This lustre pottery, some of the best of which was being produced around the time of the Granada war, is still made near Valencia and is one of the outstanding legacies of Mudéjar, or as it is more usually called Hispano-Moresque, art. Originally the technique of using an iridescent metallic sheen was developed in Persia, Mesopotamia and Egypt, but it was perfected in Spain by the tenth century and for a while established principally at Málaga. Spanish *azulejos* are of course also still famous, and *azulejos* are main features of the Alhambra and the Alcázar at Seville. The Mudéjares also excelled as ivory carvers, gold and silver smiths, and brass founders, and their work can be seen especially in the treasuries of many Spanish cathedrals.

The great cathedrals of Spain were largely built under the influence of French Gothic, but Mudéjar workmen were used on many smaller churches, which thus show a blend of Muslim and Christian features. The Chapel of the Annunciation in Sigüenza Cathedral (1510) is a superb example of Mudéjar motifs mixed with Florentine Renaissance. In Aragon the Mudéjar church towers are often detached from the main buildings like minarets, and have coloured tiles and brick patterns, such as would have been seen all over pre-Christian Granada. The finest of these was the leaning tower of Zaragoza, built in 1504 but pulled down in 1894. And nobody today, after seeing the stalactite ceilings of the Alhambra and the *media naranja* (half orange) ceiling in the Hall of the Ambassadors in

Seville, would be surprised to learn that, with lustre pottery, ceiling construction is one of the most important of the Spanish minor arts inherited from the Mudéjares.

The Muslims who had followed Boabdil into the Alpujarras set about irrigating the valleys and intensifying the cultivation of silkworms. Others worked hard to restore the ruined Vega to its former lush productivity. Here there was some conflict with the Christian immigrants who soon outnumbered the Mudéjares. The new archbishop of Granada was Hernando de Talavera, a saintly character. He, the Count of Tendilla and the royal secretary, Fernando de Zafra, tried gently to persuade the Mudéjares to accept Christian ways and the Christian faith. However, there was soon evidence that any fresh converts were secretly carrying on with their old religion. This 'loss of souls' grieved the Catholic Kings, and there was alarm about the activity of *monfíes* or bandits in the mountains coupled with the activity of North African pirates along the coast. As Muslims were for the time being exempt from the Inquisition, it was decided to send to Granada the ascetic new primate of Spain, Cardinal Ximénez de Cisneros.

The cardinal now issued an edict for forcible baptisms and had eighty thousand books in Arabic publicly burnt. There was immediate panic in the Albaicín followed by a revolt, which soon spread into the Alpujarras, with an appeal for help to Egypt. The Spaniards reacted savagely, and the rebels were suppressed, although there was an even more serious revolt in the mountains near Ronda. As a result, in February 1502, an edict was issued closely modelled on that against the Jews: the Mudéjares had two months to decide between conversion and expulsion. In point of fact it turned out to be practically impossible for them to leave the country. Ximénez now proceeded with his mass baptisms, and in the royal chapel in Granada there is a contemporary relief showing sanctimonious tonsured priests pouring water on the heads of humble Muslims. This choice of baptism or exile was extended throughout Castile but not enforced in Aragon until 1525 – a blow at landowners who had relied on Muslim slave labour. In theory therefore there were no more Muslims or Mudéjares left in Spain. These Christianized Muslims became known as Moriscos.

After Isabel's death the heir to Castile was her daughter Juana *la Loca* (the Mad), married to Philip the Handsome, who acted as regent until his death in 1506, when Fernando took over the regency. Fernando died in 1516, and the new king of the united Spain and of the vast new territories of the New World was Charles I, son of Juana and Philip, through whom as a Hapsburg he also became Holy Roman Emperor and better known

44. *A rare* azulejo, *or glazed tile, showing the arms of the Nasrid sultans entwined in the foliage and arabesques (left)*

45. *An example of silk woven in Granada in the fifteenth century (right)*

therefore as the Emperor Charles V. This was the beginning of the greatest period in Spain's history.

As the years went by it became once more obvious that the so-called Moriscos in Granada were hardly conforming at all. The women in particular wore traditional dress – long veils, baggy trousers and short tunics – and dyed their finger-ends. A bad example was also set by the converted Jews who had rushed to settle in Granada in order to escape the Inquisition. Therefore in 1525 Charles V reaffirmed the old decree, the choice again being full genuine conversion or expulsion from Spain. In 1526 the Inquisition was set up in Granada and *autos de fe* began. It was again a time of alarms about Muslim encroachment in Europe, for the Turks were soon to reach Vienna, the heart of the empire.

Charles V spent his honeymoon in the Alhambra. New apartments were built around the Garden of Lindaraxa, with paintings of grotesques and a representation of the emperor's victory over the pirate Barbarossa at Tunis by artists supposedly the pupils of Raphael. A delightful little mirador, decorated with frescoes, was constructed above a tower to be known afterwards as the Peinador or Tocador de la Reina, since it was used as the empress's boudoir; it still has a perforated marble slab through

46. *Philip II, who was responsible for the final expulsion of the Moors from Spain*

47. *Don John of Austria,*
commander-in-chief of
the Spanish forces in
Granada from 1568

which scents were said to have drifted 'to fumigate the person'. Charles also restored the sultan's baths for his personal use, putting in new tiles, and converted the Mexuar or viziers' council-chamber into a chapel. But, above all, he caused to be constructed a huge new Renaissance palace adjoining the Courts of the Myrtles and the Lions.

The palace of Charles V has often been attacked as being incongruous and overpowering, yet in itself it is a magnificent and important piece of architecture. Charles wished to reserve the old Alhambra buildings for himself and his wife, and it was therefore necessary for him to add a building for official functions – and this building had to be worthy of an emperor. Moreover he needed to clear away an area of slum buildings outside.

The architect chosen was Pedro Machucha, who had studied under Raphael, and the Bramante-like palace, a soft caramel brown, was designed as a huge square, elaborately and beautifully sculpted around the doorways, with a circular courtyard inside, surrounded by an arcade with thirty-six Doric columns, and with thirty-six more Ionic columns above. A grand approach was laid out starting from the town with a triumphal arch, the Puerta de las Granadinas, and leading up the hill through the shady *alamedas*, full of rushing streams from the Alhambra fountains. In

48. *The fountain in the Court of the Lions, which was restored to its medieval shape in 1966*

point of fact the palace was left unfinished and only finally roofed over in this century. It is indeed a contrast, and a fairly dramatic one, to the rest of the Alhambra, but dramatic contrasts in architectural styles are something one has to get used to in many cities, in London for instance. The demolishing of the Alhambra's mosque towards the end of the century was, however, particularly to be regretted, especially since its replacement, the Church of Santa María, is – frankly – dull.

In 1566 there were new decrees against the Moriscos, such as the banning of the veil for women, the seizing of books in Arabic and the closure of public baths, which were regarded as places for secret Muslim rituals and sexual promiscuity. Two years later, on Christmas Eve, a rebellion that was to be far more violent than the first broke out in the Alpujarras. It was a rebellion that grew out of despair, because of the Inquisition and the confiscation of properties, and because of the autocratic behaviour of the Church. There had been a ban on the export of silk from Granada, followed by some drastic increases in taxes on silk products. All this had resulted in destitution. When fighting got under way, the cruelty was horrible on both sides. The mountain men desecrated churches, killed and tortured priests. The Spaniards were in the end ordered to kill all prisoners, including women and children. In

49. *The Patio de la Sultana in the Generalife*

Granada itself, a Christian mob broke into the gaol and massacred all the Morisco prisoners.

There had been plenty of warnings about a probable irruption, but the new king, Philip II, had been too preoccupied with his war in Flanders. In actual fact this war could not have come at a worse time for Spain, especially as the Turkish fleet was increasing in the eastern Mediterranean. At first the commander of the Spanish forces was the Marquis of Mondéjar, grandson of the old Count of Tendilla and now hereditary governor of the Alhambra. Philip II was suspicious of his reputation of softness towards the Moriscos, and made him share the command with his rival, the Marquis de los Vélez, a more ruthless character. Such a combination was of course doomed, so in due course they were made to hand over to Philip II's half-brother, Don John of Austria, whose inexperience led to further disasters and expense.

A king, of the blood of the Prophet and descended from the caliphs of Córdoba, was proclaimed in the Alpujarras: Fernando de Valor, who took the Arab name of Aben Humeya. But 'greed was at the root of him', and within a year he was strangled by his followers. His place as king was taken by a cousin, Aben Aboó, and the dance of death became ever more grisly. Although the Turks failed to exploit the uprising, many Turkish mercenaries joined the rebels, as did others from the Barbary coast. When all was lost, Aben Aboó was murdered in a cave and his body stuffed with straw. His head was cut off by the Spaniards and stuck on one of Granada's gates.

Philip II now decided that the only solution to the problem of the Moriscos was to uproot the majority of them from the original sultanate, and resettle them in the north of Spain. This he proceeded to do, and in return some fifty thousand settlers from Galicia, León and Asturias were brought down to fill the gaps that had thus been left. Those Moriscos who

50. *A priest attempting to convert the Moors to Christianity*

remained were by and large experts in the silk industry, but before long virtually all of them had been expelled from the city of Granada. It is not surprising that the history of this last desperate revolt, written by Don Diego Hurtado de Mendoza, the uncle of the Marquis of Mondéjar, was suppressed as being too critical of the Spanish government.

The final act in the persecution of the Moriscos was yet to come. By 1600, in spite of the Christian victory over the Turks at the battle of Lepanto, there were new fears of Turkish attacks. The resettled Moriscos were proving unassimilable and many had gravitated to towns, where they were unpopular with local people. There was also concern because of the greater birthrate in some areas among Moriscos than Christians. The weak Spanish government, anxious for easy popularity, decided on the forcible expulsion of the Moriscos from Spain, and this was put into effect between 1609 and 1614. Some records say that nearly half a million left, but the more likely figure appears to be two hundred and seventy-five thousand, out of some three hundred thousand.

Like the Jews in 1492, many died of exposure, disease and starvation on their journeys to the sanctuary of Muslim lands. Fourteen hundred paid large sums for permits to enter France, but were turned away at the frontier. The tragedy was that many found it hard to settle even among co-religionists. Again like the Sephardic Jews, they took a pride in their Spanish ancestry and considered themselves to be of superior stock. A great many went to Tunisia, and a group settled at what is now known as Rabat, forming their own republic. Several of the Moriscos joined the corsairs and thus took their revenge on the Christians.

Traces of old Muslim traditions are easily recognizable to this day in Andalusia. Until recently in some remote areas, and even in the tourist 'paradise' of Mojacar near Almería, there were peasant women who went veiled, and in the Alpujarras, as Gerald Brenan has described, there is a strong Morisco atmosphere. A great number of words in the Spanish language are of Arab origin. Present-day Spaniards indeed like to joke that they are one quarter Arab, one quarter Jew and two quarters mad Christian.

To lose such a large section of its most industrious inhabitants was a disaster for Spain, on top of the large emigrations to the New World. The seventeenth century turned out to be a century of swift decline in Spanish power. In the succeeding centuries Muslims of Spanish ancestry continued to dream of returning to Granada, their paradise on earth. In *Don Quixote* the Morisco Ricote is made to say: 'Wherever we are, we weep for Spain, for after all, there we were born, and it is our natural fatherland.'

73

CHAPTER V

The passion for tales of chivalry and romance continued in Spain throughout the sixteenth century, and the 'Moorish novel' became as much a typical Spanish genre as the picaresque. The noble clan of the Abencerrajes and the Princess Lindaraxa, always of peerless beauty, featured in most of the books, usually to the detriment of poor Boabdil, and to the confusion of historical fact. In those novels the Abencerrajes were the opponents of Boabdil, whose wife – also of amazing beauty – was, if not faithless, at least tempted by adultery.

The first known edition of Montalvo's revision of the medieval romance *Amadís de Gaula*, once as popular as the Arthurian legends, was in 1508. In his preface he said that it had been inspired by the chivalric deeds during the siege of Granada. The ballads and *Amadís* were the great influences behind the creation of *Don Quixote*. Mariana's history of Spain, often rising to epic heights, was written first in Latin, and he admitted that he had often put down more than he believed. Otherwise the main author connected with the heady legends of the Alhambra was Ginés Pérez de Hita, whose *Guerras Civiles de Granada* was more of a historical novel than a history, and was interspersed with ancient and newly composed ballads, including perhaps the most genuinely moving of them all, which most Spanish children learn: on the death of 'Abenámar' before the battle of La Higueruela. In this book we have every popular guidebook's favourite of the many stories of the slaughter of the Abencerrajes in the Alhambra, when Boabdil is told by the chief of the Zegris that his lovely sultana Zoraïde is apt to 'enjoy lustful passion' beneath a rosebush in the Generalife gardens with the Abencerraje Albin Hamet. To this day one is shown the indelible bloodstains where Albin Hamet and thirty-five of his followers were beheaded. And the trysting-place of the lovers is said to be in the Patio de los Cipreses in the Generalife, indeed a romantically snug place, with a pool into which fountain jets softly trickle, and surrounded by luxuriant and scented shrubs. Pérez de Hita's work was also the inspiration for Dryden's tragedy *The Conquest of Granada*, first performed in 1672, featuring of course Lindaraxa, though Albin Hamet had turned into 'Almanzor' and Zoraïde had become 'Almahide', a part played by Nell Gwyn.

51. *Silk cloth woven by the Moors in the thirteenth or fourteenth centuries*

In sixteenth-century music Juan Vásquez was the major figure in the Andalusian school, and many of his love lyrics are still sung, particularly *De los álamos vengo* (I come from the poplars), a favourite of García Lorca. Spanish children also still learn a song by an anonymous writer of the period, *Tres moriscas m'enamoran* (Three Moorish girls are in love with me), composed for the vihuela, an especially popular instrument at the time of Queen Isabel.

In 1591 a gunpowder explosion severely damaged the Alhambra. There were also earthquakes on occasions, and in 1633 the unfinished palace of Charles V had finally to be abandoned. Nevertheless the Alhambra buildings were kept in some repair, though Richard Ford said in his *Hand-Book* that they were turned into an 'asylum for debtors' and later used for 'invalid soldiers, prisoners and convicts'. The Catholic Kings, as we know from the German traveller Münzer, made an effort to restore the Generalife, which in due course became the tenancy of the Marquises of Campotéjar, descended not only from the Bannigas clan, ancient foes of the Abencerrajes, but from Aben Hud, who had opposed the first Nasrid king Muhammed I. In the late sixteenth century this family was presumably responsible for the Renaissance mirador and flight of steps which now help to make the Patio de los Cipreses an even more enchanted spot. In due course, however, the Generalife went by descent to the Grimaldis and Pallavicinis of Genoa – not, as it turned out, particularly energetic stewards.

Here, in passing, one must mention the creation of another building in Granada in the seventeenth century which in its fantastic richness and florid ornamentation, almost bewildering, obviously owes something to the Alhambra's proximity: the Cartuja. Indeed the sacristy, in the style known as Churrigueresque, is like a mad challenge to Moorish decorative art and architecture.

Next in the story comes Isabel of Parma, queen of Philip V. She loved the Alhambra, and the couple used the old royal apartments overlooking the garden of Lindaraxa. The stalactites of the ceiling of the Room of the Mocárabes, which leads into the Court of the Lions, had been damaged by the explosion of 1591, so were replaced in their honour with a Baroque ceiling. It is pleasant to imagine the grand and handsome Isabel enjoying the quiet in the Peinador de la Reina, which hangs, as Washington Irving says, like a bird-cage above the valley of the Darro.

Unfortunately for posterity, the Marquis of Mondéjar, descendant of the Count of Tendilla of *Reconquista* days, had supported the Hapsburgs against Philip V, a Bourbon, and now had his hereditary post as governor

52. *An engraving by Gustave Doré of the Darro river which flows through Granada, separating the hill of the Alhambra from the Albaicín*

53. *The Court of the Lions showing the fountain and water courses*

of the Alhambra removed from him. In a rage the marquis ripped down his Moorish palace, which in 1494 Münzer had described as the most magnificent of all the palaces in the Alhambra. This was the beginning of a general deterioration, described so scathingly by Ford, although in the 1770s General Ricardo Wall, who – in spite of being Irish – had been minister under Charles III, did put some disfiguring red tiles on the roofs around the Court of the Lions.

Spain in the seventeenth century seemed something of a world apart to the rest of Europe, in spite of its great literature, the golden age of which is reckoned to have ended with the death of Calderón in 1681. Among the few foreign travellers who wrote memoirs were two enthusiasts, Madame d'Aulnoy and Lady Fanshaw. According to Ford, people began

54. *Families living and working in the Tower of the Infantas.*
   A water-colour by J. F. Lewis, 1833

carving their initials on the Alhambra's walls in about 1670. The spate of British travel-books about Spain date from about a hundred years later, the first writer of note to mention the Alhambra being Richard Twiss in 1773. By then Andalusia was notorious for its bandits and one was advised to travel with a military escort. Twiss also met the writer Padre Juan de Echevarría, who with Pérez de Hita was responsible for many of the fantasies about the Alhambra. One of the most attractive eighteenth-century travel writers about Spain was Henry Swinburne, whose book was published in 1779 and is full of anecdotes and good descriptions of the Alhambra, even if he found Granada itself, with its fifty thousand inhabitants, filthy and poor. Other books on Spain by Joseph Townsend and Robert Southey were published in 1791 and 1797. For Southey his journey to Spain was an important experience and it led among other things to translations of Spanish ballads, and of the *Chronicle of the Cid* and *Amadís de Gaula*.

In due course translated versions of Spanish ballads were also written by Thomas Rodd, John Bowring, Lockhart, Ticknor and Byron. However, the vision of Spain both as a land of chivalry and a model of Christian virtues had already taken root in Germany, following a more tenebrous picture of the country in Goethe's *Egmont* and Schiller's *Don Carlos*. August Wilhelm von Schlegel published translations of ballads and – in particular – of the plays of Calderón, the latter becoming a cult and produced by Hoffmann at Bamberg. His brother Friedrich von Schlegel published a full-length Spanish *ritterdrama* called *Alarcos* in 1802. To Hegel the Spanish ballads were like 'a string of pearls'. Ludwig Tieck translated *Don Quixote*; Clemens Brentano wrote a poem entitled *Alhambra*; Fouqué in 1805 wrote the *Ballad of Roncesvalles*; Heine was to write a poem called *Almansor*. There were also many important critical works on Spanish literature.

From William Jacob we learn that in 1809 French prisoners of war were being kept in the Alhambra, and also that an earthquake had practically ruined Santa Fe. Ford was to write angrily about the five daughters of the governor Bucarelli, who not only stripped off *azulejos* and sold them in Granada (once to pay for a bull-fight) but used the exquisite Hall of the Two Sisters as a 'silk manufactory', filling it with looms. Then came another 'family of caterpillars', followed by the regime of Don Ignacio Montilla, whose wife kept a donkey in the Mexuar and sheep in the patio outside. All this did not prevent James Cavanah Murphy from making exact and often beautiful architectural drawings (though despised by Ford) between 1802 and 1809 for his *Arabian Antiquities of Spain*, published eventually in 1815 at huge cost.

Jacob and Murphy had to leave Spain hurriedly as the French army advanced south under Marshal Soult, who proceeded to amass one of the greatest private collections of Spanish pictures ever known, acquired either from Andalusian churches or as a ransom for noble prisoners. Other French generals had their collections of pictures and church plate, including the Corsican Sébastiani at Granada. Under Sébastiani some repairs were done at the Alhambra and gardens laid out, but any good was nullified by his depredations in the town, the axing of the elms in the Alameda (replaced by the Duke of Wellington, according to Ford), and above all the destruction of eight of the Alhambra's towers when the French had to withdraw in September 1812. More towers would have

55. *'Modern Christians in the palaces of the ancient Moorish kings.'An engraving by Doré showing tourists collecting souvenirs*

disappeared but for the bravery of a Spanish soldier, José García, who cut the fuses for the explosives.

The five years' campaign in the Peninsula saw some vicious fighting, but the spell of Spain – its landscape and its people, its grandeur and its tragedy, its history and its customs, its gaiety and its cruelty – had an effect on the imagination of the invaders and was finally to blaze into full Romantic glory a decade and a half later. Gone was the time when Chateaubriand could dismiss the Alhambra with a few words; in 1826 there appeared his *Le Dernier des Abencérages*. Spain had also become 'Oriental'. Victor Hugo, like George Sand, had spent some of his childhood in Madrid, his father having been a general. In 1829 the *Orientales* were published, and soon Granada became '*le capital du monde romantique*' in the words of the Marquis de Custine.

56. *The Casa Sánchez in the Alhambra. The Fords were among the tourists who rented Yusuf III's charming little garden palace before it was restored to its former glory*

57. *A view of the Comares tower and the Hall of the Ambassadors from the Tocador de la Reina. A coloured drawing by Richard Ford, 1831*

But first there were more sedate French travellers, such as Bourgoing and Laborde, who wrote painstaking books with nonetheless enticing engravings. There was also a spate of military memoirs and letters from the British, lasting until the 1830s. Byron's first cantos of *Childe Harold* had come out in 1812 – 'O lovely Spain, renown'd romantic land!' Lord Porchester's poem *The Moor* with its lengthy notes once more stirred up legends of Zegris, Albin Hamet and the like. In 1829 the Polish Adam Mickiewicz wrote a ballad called *Alpujarra*, about revenge. In this the Muslim Alman Zor kisses the leader of the Christian forces and then tells him, 'I have the plague. This is my revenge.' 'Plague in Granada' is still a common phrase in Poland.

As a reward for the battle of Salamanca the Duke of Wellington was presented with the estate of Soto de Roma (Grove of Pomegranates) outside Granada. In Charles III's time it had originally been given to General Wall, and had then been passed by Charles IV to 'the minion Godoy' (Ford). The estate, with Molino del Rey (Mill of the King), had fine vineyards and plantations of olives and mulberries, but the duke never went there, neither did his successors until 1906. The first agent was one of his aides, General O'Lawlor, again Irish, who was also Captain-General of Granada when Washington Irving came in 1828 and 1829.

Other Americans had fallen in love with Spain – Ticknor, Longfellow and Bayard Taylor. To Ticknor the Alhambra was 'a name to make my blood thrill if I live to the frosts of a century'. It is sad for us that a book so freshly written as *A Year in Spain* 'by a young American' (i.e. Alexander Slidell) did not include Granada; he was one of the many who became fascinated not only by the *fiestas de toro* and the fandangos, but by the notorious bandits, *bandoleros*, who lurked like Robin Hoods or Dick Turpins in the rugged and fearsome mountains of Andalusia.

Washington Irving was already renowned as the creator of Rip Van Winkle, Knickerbocker and Squire Bracebridge. In 1829 his *Conquest of Granada* was published, full of hard research and praised by Coleridge as his *chef d'œuvre*, but spoiled by the introduction of a fictional and irritatingly garrulous priest-historian, Fray Antonio Agapida. Irving came for the second time to Granada with the Russian Prince Dolgorouki, who presented the Visitors' Book that is still in the Alhambra library, in the hope that it might deter people from writing their names on walls (Irving found Chateaubriand's near the Peinador, and Henry Swinburne wrote verses in the Baths). They were lucky enough to be lent part of the governor's apartments above the Mexuar.

David Wilkie had advised his friend Irving to write something in the 'Haroun Alraschid style', with a dash of Arabian spice. Luckily for us Irving wrote a quite different type of book. The pleasure in reading *The Alhambra*, published in 1832, is not only in the Moorish legends, which so often begin with the familiar 'Once upon a time', but in the sheer happiness and delight that emanate from it. The book is repetitive and on occasions absurd, but it is natural and friendly. There is also the affection for the simple but proud denizens of the crumbling Alhambra – Tía Antonia, her niece Dolores, the bottle-nosed old fellow 'as poor as a rat' but who grandly called himself Alonso de Aguilar, and above all the chattering Mateo Ximénez (another grand name), a true *hijo de la Alhambra* (son of the Alhambra). In due course Irving discovered those 'mysterious chambers' where he went to live alone among bats and owls:

84

in point of fact the Sala de las Frutas in Charles V's apartments, where Isabel of Parma had also stayed. He loved to sit in the Peinador of an evening, watching the shadows; and in the morning he would go to the window in the Tower of Comares, which as he says he used as a kind of observatory, listening to the 'click of castanets' and the 'dubious tone of the guitar', in the very place where Charles V made that much quoted remark, 'Ill-fated was the man who lost all this!' 'I have never had such a delicious abode,' Irving wrote to Dolgorouki, by now in Madrid. 'One of my windows looks into the little garden of Lindaraxa; the citron trees are full of blossom and perfume the air . . .'

58. *The young Washington Irving, author of* The Conquest of Granada *and* Legends of the Alhambra

His story of the three infantas is perhaps the best known: how they fell in love with three handsome Christian captives, and how two of them eloped with the aid of their duenna, but the third was too fluttery and timid to climb down the rope ladder and so remained to pine alone in her 'silken chamber' and eventually became its ghost. *A Ramble among the Hills* is one of the most memorable chapters, when Mateo tells him about the ghost of the headless horse and the pot of Moorish gold, and when they see the evening star above the Sierra Nevada – 'If I could get it,' Irving said, 'I would cut it up into diamonds, for all the ladies of Granada.' After four months Washington Irving left, reluctantly, for a post in the Legation in London. 'Thus ended one of the pleasantest dreams of my life, which the reader may think has been but too much made up of dreams.'

59. *A chat round the brasero, by John Phillip (1866). This painting is a good example of* costumbrismo *in the art of the period*

CHAPTER VI

Washington Irving said that he used to tell stories to the two-year-old Eugénie de Montijo, future Empress of France. She had been born prematurely in Granada during an earthquake, on 5 May 1826. Her mother was Scottish, born María Manuela Kirkpatrick, the daughter of a wine merchant in Málaga. Charles Rochfort Scott, on tour from the Gibraltar garrison, described meeting this lady who wore a green sash with the daring words *Constitución o muerte* (Constitution or death) on it; for she was a confirmed hater of the absolute regime of Ferdinand VII, not only for political reasons but because the king had dared to complain about her husband, then Count de Teba, marrying a foreign commoner.

In 1830 the countess was in Madrid, and met Prosper Mérimée on his way north from Granada. There was an immediate affinity between them. 'Do you remember', he wrote years later, 'all the stories you used to tell me about the Alhambra and the Generalife? I am sure that with you I saw the enchanted Moor that I vainly tried to evoke in the Mirador de la Reina.' It is also clear that it was she who gave him the germ of an idea for his immortal *Carmen*.

The novel was published in 1846 and the première of Bizet's opera was in 1875, five years after Mérimée's death. In 1825, without even having visited Spain, he had written his *Théâtre de Clara Gazul*, dramatic pieces attributed to an imaginary Spanish comedienne. Musset's *Contes d'Espagne* was another milestone in the Romantic cult of Spain, and Mérimée finally left Paris for Spain after the uproar between Classicists and Romantics over the performance of Victor Hugo's *Hernani*, partly set in Zaragoza. Mérimée was fascinated by Andalusia, and was to write quantities of articles about Spanish art, theatre, literature and customs. Between 1831 and 1833 he wrote five brilliant 'letters' about Spain for the *Revue de Paris*. The third of these was about the bandits of Andalusia, and in this he spoke of the famous José María, the *bandolero* chief who operated between Seville and Granada, always dressed in splendid *majo* costumes, and so courteous that he would first kiss a lady's hand before taking off her ring. This José María, known as *el Tempranillo* (the Early One) was eventually a model for José Navarro in *Carmen*. According to Custine, however, José María was not averse to chopping off fingers if he wanted rings in a hurry.

60. *A drawing by Lewis of the bandit, José María, 'a fine handsome fellow and fit to be absolute king of Andalusia'*

Every traveller at this period wrote of the perils of the Andalusian bandits (Spanish bandits, along with the Inquisition, had featured in M. G. Lewis's very popular Gothic novel *The Monk*, published in 1796), but those were not the only problems of wayfaring. The country inns or *ventas* were extremely primitive, and usually sleep would be impossible because of what Henry Inglis, author of *Spain in 1830*, called the unrelenting attacks of 'certain enemies of repose whose name might be called "legion" '. Disraeli had some alarms about bandits when journeying to Granada, but enjoyed the excitement of it. A Sephardic Jew, he looked so southern and so much at home as he paced the halls of the Alhambra that the old lady who showed him round kept asking if he was a Moor, a *dernier Abencérage* no doubt. *'Es mi casa'*, 'It is my house', he eventually told her as he left, and she was satisfied.

Contrary to expectations, Disraeli found the Alhambra in relatively good order and not a ruin, 'scarcely in a state of dilapidation', and Rochfort Scott was pleased to find that the Court of the Lions had been greatly cleared up since his last visit ten years before. In those days the lions had been swamped in a flowery jungle of sunflowers, larkspurs and marigolds. Now, in military parlance, it was 'in perfect inspection order', and pillars had been scrubbed to remove names and doggerel verses. Doubtless Disraeli's old lady was Irving's Tía Antonia, whose real name was Francisca de Molina, and it was she who had done the scrubbing.

In 1832 Irving's *Alhambra* was published and at once received with immense enthusiasm in Britain and America, and was soon translated into other languages. Thackeray compared Irving to Goldsmith and called him 'one of the most charming masters of our lighter language'. So Spain also became the domain of the bourgeois, so much despised by the French Romantics, and Seville tailors were kept busy making *majo* costumes for English tourists.

Richard Ford, with his attractive wife Harriet and four children, first came to Granada in June 1831, after staying in Seville in the house of the connoisseur Hall Standish. They travelled by way of Jaén, luckily untroubled by bandits and through fantastic scenery, with 'torrents, rivers, rocks, precipices, goats, vines, figs, lights and shades', but 'wanting in good accommodation for man or beast'. At last they reached the fabled city, 'such a profusion of trees and water'. 'Here we are,' he wrote to the British Minister Addington, 'with the most delicious breezes from the snowy mountains above, perfumed by a thousand groves and gardens of vine, orange and pomegranate, carolled by nightingales.' On Irving's recommendation, he managed to secure accommodation within

61. *The apartments above the Mexuar patio where Ford and his family had lodgings. A drawing by Harriet Ford*

62. *The road to Granada from Jaén. 'The gorge became wilder and narrower and is tunnelled at Puerto de Arenas.' A water-colour and gouache by Richard Ford*

the Alhambra, namely in the governor's apartments above the Mexuar. The times were, however, particularly troubled. Shortly before his arrival there had been the horrifying execution of a young widow soon to be a national heroine, Mariana de Pineda, who had been garrotted for possessing a flag with the Constitutional colours.

Ford's opinion of the state of the Alhambra was far different from Disraeli's, and his stay was not improved by the clanking of the chains of galley-slaves, who were converting part of the buildings into storehouses for salted fish and in the process sending bits of Moorish stucco flying down the precipices. A crumbling staircase led from his apartments into the Hall of the Ambassadors; gunpowder was kept in the palace of Charles V, which did not even have a lightning conductor. Nevertheless he came to know and love every corner of the Alhambra's palaces, taking careful notes and sketching views and features. These notes were to be the basis of part of his *Hand-Book*, regarded not only as a model for all future guidebooks to any country but outstanding as travel literature, with a real, deep affection for Spain. He travelled all over the peninsula, at least two thousand miles in all; and he made an important collection of Spanish pictures, though he did not share the enthusiasm of Hugo and Gautier for Goya. In Seville he missed Delacroix, who however saw Harriet, but he became friendly with J. F. Lewis, who gave Harriet drawing lessons. Also whilst in Seville he actually met the bandit José María, who came to see him. 'The whole town is talking,' Ford told Addington. 'I received him as a man of his merit deserves and gave him a present of a pistol, with which probably if he meets me on the high road he will shoot me. Lewis, who is with me still, made a drawing of him – a fine handsome fellow and fit to be absolute King of Andalusia.'

Lewis stayed with the Fords on their third stay in the Alhambra in 1833. By then they were living in the Casa Sánchez, the ramshackle building that was the Palace of the Partal no less and now usually known as the Tower of Las Damas, with its superb view of the Peinador, the Generalife and the Albaicín, but with the great pool before it still empty, ever since the water supply had been blown up by the French. In many ways Ford's descriptions of the Alhambra are the opposite to Irving's – factual, realistic, though with some high-flown passages. He even warns against disappointments and the 'nonsense' of 'over-exaggerated notions'. 'Few airy castles of illusion will stand the test of reality . . . But to understand the Alhambra, it must be lived in . . . At twilight it becomes a vision of the past, for daylight dispels the dreamy haunted air, and we begin to

3. *Three studies of Richard Ford in Spanish dress by Joaquín Becquer.*
   Costumbrismo *was a cult among tourists of the period*

examine, measure, criticize . . .' 'It must be lived in' – yes, indeed, but for us a hundred and fifty years later such possibilities are long past.

Ford had a dry humour, but some of his observations about the Spaniards, and especially the Granadinos, 'stagnating in bookless ignorance', do seem excessively caustic at times. But he was exasperated by their apparent disdain of the Alhambra and hoped that his words would spur them into some sort of interest in their unique heritage. The first edition of his *Hand-Book* had actually to be withdrawn because of some over-strong criticisms, but the second edition in 1845 was a great success. In the following year Murray published Ford's *Gatherings from Spain*, partly made up from introductory material for the original *Hand-Book*. He contributed regularly to the Edinburgh *Quarterly Review*, writing many articles on Spanish subjects and reviewing on their publication Borrow's *The Bible in Spain* and Prescott's *Ferdinand and Isabella*. David Roberts referred to Ford's accurate drawings when preparing his *Picturesque Sketches in Spain* (1837), and other drawings were engraved as illustrations for *Childe Harold* and Lockhart's *Spanish Ballads*.

Lewis made about fifty studies of the Alhambra, and earned himself the title of 'Spanish Lewis'. Later he turned his attention to the Near East and became the leading English Orientalist painter, admired by Ruskin and Gautier. David Roberts just missed his friend at the Alhambra and was equally captivated by it, though he spent more time in Seville. He had come to Spain to find material for illustrated albums, and on his return worked up his sketches as well as making finished oil paintings of Spanish scenes, which earned him enough money to travel to the eastern Mediterranean. His sense of drama and imaginative use of light and shade made him into the first artist of importance to respond in the Romantic manner to the Moorish architecture of Spain; it also prepared him for the great set-pieces of Eastern subjects that brought him such fame.

The new *sevillano* school of artists obviously owed much to British influence, both directly from Roberts and Lewis and indirectly from Turner, John Martin and others. The most outstanding of those artists, who included Barrón, Cortés, the Dominguez Bécquers and Esquivel, was Jenaro Pérez Villaamil, a Galician by origin. He had met Roberts in Granada and was also a friend of the Spanish Romantic writer *par excellence*, the prolific José Zorrilla, who was responsible for presenting the Don Juan legend in perhaps its most popular form, in his swash-buckling play *Don Juan Tenorio*. For it had not been long before foreign Romanticism in Spain had produced a native Spanish Romanticism, and this – as a revolutionary movement – had even for a while been associated with liberalism. Zorrilla wrote many poems, including the 'Oriental

64. *Harriet Ford in the dress of a* maja *with 'four million filigree buttons'. Painting by R. R. Reinagle after a print by J. F. Lewis*

poem' *Granada* (1852) and *Boabdil* – 'O Lady in the dark head-dress, gladly would I give you Granada just for one kiss', etc.

Another Andalusian dramatist was Antonio García Gutiérrez whose *El Trovador* (1836) and *Simón Bocanegra* (1843) were made famous by Verdi's operas. The Duke of Rivas' narrative poem *El moro expósito* (1834) was in

65. *The pool of the Partal and the Tower of Las Damas, formerly the Casa Sánchez where the Fords lodged in the summer of 1833 (see page 82)*

the Walter Scott tradition, and had an introduction by Alcalá-Galiano which is generally regarded as the Spanish Romantic manifesto. He also wrote ballads and a drama in verse and prose, *Don Alvaro o la Fuerza del Sino*, which provided a libretto for *La Forza del Destino*.

A particular offshoot of Spanish Romanticism was *costumbrismo*, the cult of local customs and manners, and here Lewis no doubt had some early impact on the artists of Seville. It was also soon found that English visitors were ready purchasers of pictures of tavern scenes, gypsies dancing, bandits in caves, and lovely girls being serenaded with guitars. From these *cuadros* (paintings) *de costumbres* there developed the *novelas* (novels) *de costumbres*, mostly of course by Andalusian authors. In effect the climax of this realistic writing came towards the end of the century with the books of Benito Pérez Galdós, born in the Canaries, who compares with Balzac and Dickens.

94

66. *Murillo's portrait of Fernando III,* conqueror of Seville,
who was later canonised

Like Ford, there were, however, other British travellers on the lookout
for old master paintings, one being Sir William Eden, and another Samuel
E. Cook, author of *Sketches of Spain* (a book again disliked by Ford). For
seven years after the death of Ferdinand VII in 1833 – during the first
Carlist War – Spain was often a dangerous place for travellers. Still, it did
not deter George Borrow, travelling on behalf of the British and Foreign

Bible Society. Alas, however, Borrow's picaresque adventures did not include Andalusia, but his *Zincali, or The Gypsies of Spain* and *The Bible in Spain* were both to take the reading public by storm. Owen Jones and Jules Goury were in the Alhambra in 1834, making drawings and taking casts. There was a cholera epidemic, and in August Goury died, but in 1842 a vast folio work was published by subscription in two volumes, *Plans, Elevations, Sections and Details of the Alhambra*, based on their joint work, the illustrations reproduced by the new printing process 'litho-chrysography', using gold. The book had the highest praise from Ford and was later referred to when serious restoration work began at the Alhambra. All the same, by modern standards the colours are a bit overpowering. Owen Jones felt that Islamic art could provide inspiration for a new style of architecture that would match the achievements and aspirations of the Victorian age: a harmonious blending with the new materials of technology. In his *The Grammar of Ornament* he described the Alhambra as the very summit of perfection, comparable to the Parthenon, and he entered a design for the Army and Navy club 'in the Alhambra style'. This work resulted in a commission to build the Alhambra Court in the Crystal Palace at Sydenham in 1854. It caused a sensation, and Holman Hunt worked there when finishing his 'Christ in the Temple'.

Another lively and somewhat loquacious travel book was by George Dennis: *A Summer in Andalucía*. Travelling in 1836, he found that Irving's Mateo Ximénez was by now a famous figure in the Alhambra, recognized as the indispensable guide and purveyor of legends though hurt by Irving having called him 'simple-minded'. The Alhambra and Granada were described at length, quite wittily, and Dennis was one of the first to draw attention to the curious fifteenth-century ceiling paintings of Moorish kings and chivalric scenes in the Sala de los Reyes. He was astounded by the 'general immorality' of Andalusian women: 'I never was in the company of an Andaluza for ten minutes but the conversation was sure to turn upon *love*. . . The grand business of every Spaniard's life is love – not pure, exalted love, but a much baser passion.' One can be sure that such passages only increased the flow of tourists to Andalusia.

In that same year Baron Isidore Taylor, a Frenchman already famous as a traveller, artist and man of letters, was commissioned by King Louis-Philippe to scour Spain for old masters. He travelled with the artists Adrien Douzats and Pharamond Blanchard, both *Orientalistes*, and succeeded in collecting nearly five hundred paintings, including many by Murillo, Velázquez, Zurbarán, Ribera and Goya. It was a propitious moment for picking up bargains, with convents closing down and the Carlist War in progress. The king's *Galerie espagnole* opened in the Louvre in 1838, and soon 'all the grandeur and glory of Spanish painting was revealed to France'. Richard Ford's friend in Seville, Hall Standish, left his collection to the Gallery; Millet declared that he virtually 'lived' there, he was so enthralled; and it is generally agreed that the Goyas, particularly the *Manolas au balcon*, had a lasting effect on the young Manet, although he did not actually go to Spain until 1867. After the death of Louis-Philippe his heirs sold up the collection in London, and it was dispersed throughout the world, the ownership of some of the paintings being still unknown.

Théophile Gautier, equipped with a daguerreotype, set out for Spain in the hope of acquiring a few bargains for himself. In this he was unsuccessful, but the journey resulted in two books regarded as classics of Romantic Hispanophilia: *Tra [sic] los montes* (1843), later retitled *Voyage en Espagne*, and *España* (1845), poems. The Alhambra had been written about so many times, but he had his own brand of freshness (unlike, for once, Dumas *père* when he went there), with a wonderful gift in particular of evoking colours and light. The four nights he slept in the Alhambra were, he said, without doubt the 'most delicious in my life'. The famous lions he found more like hippopotami or chimeras, but worthy of Ibn Zamrak's poem round the fountain's rim. When the moon shone he and his friend Piot were able to face the ghosts of the beheaded Abencerrajes with plenty of bottles of sherry, chilled in the fountain. Perhaps the Generalife, where peacocks screeched on the battlements, moved him most of all. He wrote of a gigantic oleander, exploding like fireworks from the centre of a pool: 'Nothing has given me a truer sense of beauty than that oleander in the Generalife,' and he wrote a poem about it. As for Granada itself, he found it 'gay, laughing, animated', though shorn of its former splendour, and once again love seemed to be the sole occupation of its inhabitants – that and the art of doing nothing.

Easily the major historical work of the period on Spain and Granada was written by an American, who not only never went to Spain, but was nearly blind: *Ferdinand and Isabella* by William H. Prescott. The book was published in 1838 in Boston, and as his fellow New Englander and biographer Ticknor was to say, 'no work of such size and gravity had ever been so successful'. Prescott had worked on it for about ten years, with the help of researchers and secretaries, and had had some key contemporary manuscripts and transcripts sent across from Madrid, notably by Bernaldez and Oviedo. The book is still a main source of reference for any history of the Granada war and the Catholic Kings. He also had access to the library of George Ticknor, whose *History of Spanish Literature* was published in 1849. Ticknor maintained that Ford's praise this time was only 'reluctant', but the *Hand-Book* belies this.

67 & 68. *Designs from the capitals of columns in the Court of the Lions,* *from Albert Calvert's* The Alhambra, *1904*

69 & 70. *A design from the great arch at the entrance to the Court of the* *Fishpond and an ornament from one of the panels in the Court of the* *Mosque, from Owen Jones's* The Grammar of Ornament, *1868*

Meanwhile travel books proliferated. Some writers like Charles Dembroski were transported by the Alhambra ('All we need is the dance of some seductive houris to believe that we are in the paradise of Muhamet'); some like Charles Cayley, author of *Las Alforjas or the Bridle Roads of Spain* were more sceptical ('Nothing earthly can bear the fatal ordeal of a previous reputation'). That was in 1854, but by 1873 the Alhambra to Augustus Hare was the 'most perfectly beautiful place in the world'. Nearly everyone agreed that it was best to see the Alhambra in the evening when 'the flood of purple and gold ebb on the plain', or by moonlight; and as Hare wisely added (which is still true), you require many visits to understand the Alhambra properly.

The traveller, said Hare in his *Wanderings in Spain*, must be prepared to unstiffen his English backbone, 'put all false Anglican pride in his pocket, and treat every Spaniard, from the lowest beggar upwards, as his equal'. Most travel-writers described the horrors of the journeys to Granada, thumping and jolting across dusty mountain roads in diligences pulled by ten mules. They remarked on the elegance of the Granada men, on the mantillas and fans of the ladies, always in traditional black, and on the flower-filled balconies, contrasted with the extreme poverty of the Sacromonte gypsies in their caves. The name Ximénez remained a magic one for guides at the Alhambra, and old Mateo was still operating there in the 1850s, though 'a twaddling old fool' to William George Clark. Usually when travellers went to Seville they would comment on the 'cigar-rolling' girls, the *cigarreras*, prototypes of Carmen and numbering about three thousand. Their books had jaunty titles such as *Gazpacho or Summer Months in Spain, An Idle Woman in Spain* and *Anglican Innocents in Spain*. Hans Christian Andersen, an admirer of Washington Irving, visited Granada in 1861, and the Alhambra was painted by innumerable French and German artists, including in particular Dehodenq, Regnault, Bamberger, Gerhardt and Lenbach.

For many of those who had never been to Spain the very word Alhambra conjured up exotic visions. Flaubert gave the name to a luxurious dance-hall in the Champs-Elysées. There was an Alhambra Theatre in Glasgow. In 1858 the Alhambra Palace opened in Leicester Square in London, on the site of the present Odeon cinema, and presenting Howes and Cushing's American circus – trapeze artistes swung overhead while you ate and drank. The décor was more Turkish or Saracenic than 'Alhambresque', but had plenty of horseshoe arches. The Alhambra Palace turned into the Royal Alhambra Palace Music Hall, and in 1882 it was burnt down, though rebuilt in the same giddy style immediately.

Even more extraordinary, not to say exotic, was the creation – still in good order – by an Italian marchese, with the resounding name of Ferdinando Panciatichi Ximénes d'Aragona. Inspired, so it would seem, in the mid-nineteenth century by the plates in Owen Jones's volume and perhaps also by the court in the Crystal Palace, he transformed his castle at Sammezzano, in the mountains north of Florence, into an Alhambra of his own dreams, afire with colours and with a good splash of Gothic to boot. Here we have the Hall of the Peacocks, the Hall of the Mirrors, the Hall of the Lovers, complete with horseshoe arches, stalactites, columns decorated with the fleur de lys and with Saracenic capitals, elaborate marble and mosaic pavements, tiles in complicated geometric designs, and florid decorative inscriptions (in Latin or Italian, not in Arabic). Across the mountains from this faery creation, at Rocchetta near Bologna, Count Cesare Mattei indulged his own fantasies by creating an entirely new castle in a semi-Moorish style, complete with a replica of the Court of Lions.

Some while back the government in Madrid had at last awoken to the international fame of the Alhambra, and had allocated a small yearly sum for repairs, gradually increasing it, subject to wars and other upheavals. The official architects unfortunately attacked the problem of 'restoration' as zestfully as mid-nineteenth century English architects attacked country churches, and some of the damage was irreparable: old, cracked fourteenth-century *azulejos*, for instance, being replaced with nice bright new tiles – not to mention some other caprices. In 1890 much of the eastern side of the Court of the Myrtles was destroyed by fire, and was rebuilt with the addition of a fancy cupola which had to be removed in 1934. The old Moorish gateway from the Plaza de Bibarrambla – once known as the Puerta de las Orejas (Gate of the Ears) because of earrings having been torn off rich ladies' ears when a platform collapsed during a fiesta in 1621 – was removed from its ancient position in the town, eventually to be re-erected and rather forlornly hidden among the elms and chestnuts in the midst of the Alhambra's *alamedas*.

Hare wrote of the 'savage violence' of the gypsy population of Granada – 'utterly without shame' and begging in the 'most violent and most imperious tones'. The Italian Edmondo De Amicis and a friend had to run 'like schoolboys', and were chased, when they were suddenly surrounded by a mob of ragged boys, fortune-tellers and beggars. Baron Davillier in his sumptuous book *L'Espagne*, with engravings by Gustave Doré, said that the gypsy children went about stark naked and were as 'black as negroes'. But he also spoke of the gypsies' 'mobility of countenance', and how they were the 'greatest gesticulators in the world, not excepting the Neapolitans'.

71. *A priest and majos admiring the Alhambra vase. An engraving by Doré,*
who exercised artistic licence in replacing the missing wing

72. *The Hall of the Abencerrajes,*
with its superb stalactite ceiling.
A painting by David Roberts

73 & 74. *Two views of the Alhambra Anastatica in Italy. Inspired by the work of Owen Jones, Ferdinando Panciatichi Ximénes d'Aragona transformed his castle at Sammezzano into a colourful, if Gothic, version of the Alhambra in Granada*

The origin of the gypsies of Granada is obscure. Some say they arrived with the Catholic Kings in 1492. Henry Swinburne mentioned them, and so did Inglis, Gautier and Dumas. The caves of the Sacromonte were described as being like a city within a city, and their inhabitants were remarked on as often having a wild beauty, with flashing black eyes and flashing white teeth. The gypsies had their own customs and *caló* (language), and they also had an extraordinary sense of rhythm and dance. Gide wrote how in the nineties he had heard a gypsy boy sing: 'a panting, excessive, painful song, in which one felt his soul expiring every time he caught his breath . . . To hear that song again, ah, I would have travelled over three Spains.' This was *cante jondo*. Real gypsy music of course differs from the essentially melancholic Andalusian music, but the time would come when the gypsies would almost be as much a symbol of Granada as the Alhambra, and some of them would be very rich.

CHAPTER VII

The association of music with Romantic Spain in a large measure began with Italian opera, but for Parisians early in the nineteenth century there had also been the sensational performances of the guitarist Fernando Sor, the 'Paganini of the guitar', and the Andalusian tenor Manuel García, who was the father of the great opera singer Malibran. The peak of Romantic ballet was reached by Taglioni, an Italian, and her 'Sylphide' was succeeded by the more impassioned pseudo-Spanish *cachucha* danced by the Viennese Fanny Elssler. María Medina was a famous Spanish dancer, and such was the attraction of Spanish names that Mrs James of Simla, having decided to kick over the traces and be a dancer too, changed hers to Lola Montes and soared to royal patronage. The actress Josefa Vargas was half gypsy from Málaga, but her family moved near Granada. She met the future Lord Sackville in Stuttgart, and became his mistress, in due course returning to dazzle Granada with her splendid dresses and jewels. As 'Pepita' she was the grandmother of Vita Sackville-West.

It has been said that from Chopin's *Bolero* to Debussy's *Iberia* every composer had his Spanish composition. Glinka went to Granada and made friends with guitarists and local musicians. His visit resulted not only in his *Jota aragonesa* (*jota* being a dance) and other works imitating the Spanish style, but in a revived interest in Russian folk-music, much of it also with oriental roots. Liszt came to Spain in 1844 and afterwards wrote his *Spanish Rhapsody*.

In Spain quantities of light-hearted songs were composed and sung in *cafés cantantes*. There were also the *zarzuelas*, the equivalent of operettas, which in effect had their beginnings in the masques of the times of Fernando and Isabel and the seventeenth-century court entertainments by writers such as Lope de Vega. *La Paloma* by Yradier, music master to the Empress Eugénie, became internationally famous, and the toreador's *Habanera* in *Carmen* was an adaptation of another of his songs.

Carmen caused a scandal and only achieved popularity in Paris at Bizet's death on the night of its thirty-first performance. It was the culmination of the Romantic *espagnolade*, a work of genius, and when finally performed in Madrid delighted the Spaniards. Yet a gradual unease arose among musicologists and folklorists, in particular Felipe Pedrell (teacher of Falla

75. *Albert F. Calvert in Muslim dress posing for the frontispiece of his book,*
The Alhambra, *1904*

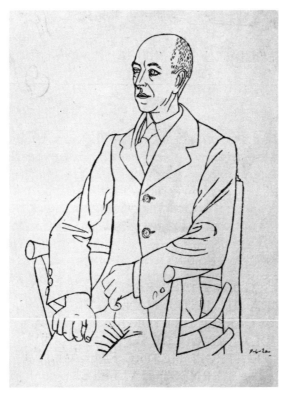

76. *A drawing of Manuel de Falla by Picasso*

and Granados, and composer of *El Ultimo Abencerraje*) who felt that *Carmen* and its imitators were giving a false image of Spain and its music. Meanwhile, the fertilising influence from France continued with pieces in mood far from the commercial music of the cafés, by Lalo, Saint-Saëns, and especially Chabrier – in that his *España* (1883) is still frequently played. The outstanding Spanish composer of the period, Albéniz, was consequently drawn to Paris, as was the violinist Sarasate, and their work created some impression. Albéniz's piano suite *Iberia* in particular influenced the young Falla. Then there were the works of composers who were not French, such as Rimsky-Korsakov's *Spanish Caprice* and Hugo Wolf's *Spanish Song-Book*.

Manuel de Falla was born in Cádiz in 1876. In Madrid his *zarzuelas* were unsuccessful, but his one-act opera *La Vida Breve*, set in Granada although he had never been there, won a prize. It was the period of the literary movement known as the Generation of '98, a time of material reassessment and examination of ancient values after Spain's war with the United States and the loss of her remaining colonies. Two names were

77. *A portrait of Federico García Lorca by Gregorio Prieto*

outstanding in this movement: Angel Ganivet, born in Granada, and Miguel de Unamuno, a Basque. Ganivet slightly anticipated it with his political novels and especially with his philosophical works *Idearium español* and *Granada la Bella*. He had written nostalgic letters from abroad about his home town to the new liberal newspaper *El Defensor de Granada*. *Granada la Bella* was a collection of essays, published in Riga where he was consul, and was the result of his alarm at hearing of the modernization of the city and of the bad taste of the new buildings. It was not, however, just a local book, evoking the charms of Granada and the Alhambra, but an attempt to stir the Granadinos, and thus the Spaniards, from a general apathy. In 1898 he drowned himself in the freezing river Dvina, and nearly thirty years later his body was brought back to Granada. His bust now stands in the Alhambra's woods.

Falla went to Paris in 1907, and almost immediately became a friend of Debussy, Ravel, Albéniz and Dukas. Debussy's *Soirée en Grenade* had appeared in 1903, causing a small uproar because of its similarity to Ravel's *Habanera*, which Ravel (half Basque) later orchestrated into his

Rhapsodie espagnole. Like Falla, Debussy had never been to Granada, and for that matter hardly to Spain, and all his inspiration came from pictures, books and the singers of Spanish folk-music in Paris. Yet he was the first to draw the true poetry in music out of Spain. Falla said that his *Iberia* (1910) was 'ideally Spanish'. When Falla finally went to Granada and sent him a postcard, it inspired Debussy to write *La Puerta del Vino*, using *cante jondo*. No doubt this card included the so-called gypsy king Chorrojumo who before the First World War was fond of posing for photographers outside the Puerta del Vino, in Moorish times the gateway between the civilian and military sections of the Alhambra.

At Granada Falla stayed at the Pensión Alhambra near the Gate of Siete Suelos, and there began making his notes for *Nights in the Gardens of Spain*. Granada cast its magic over him and he finally settled there in 1920. He was to be one of the finest Spanish composers not only of his generation but of the century.

Falla was born an Andalusian, and to him the music of Andalusia held the soul of Spain, and this music had Hispano-Arabic roots, in the old al-Andalus. In Paris he completed his *Four Spanish Pieces*, but his turning point was the performance of *La Vida Breve* at the Opéra Comique in 1913. *El Amor Brujo, Love the Magician*, was written for Pastora Imperio of the famous green eyes, one of the greatest dancers in the gypsy manner; the setting of this piece was of course Granada, and it included the now well-known *Ritual Fire Dance* as well as *cante jondo* singing. But its success only came years later. Next he completed his three nocturnes, the *Nights in the Gardens of Spain* – typically Andalusian, mixing nostalgia with rhythm – and these were followed by *The Three-Cornered Hat*, one theme of which was based on a tune he heard played by a blind man on a guitar in Granada. The ballet of *The Three-Cornered Hat* was first produced by Massine for Diaghilev in 1922, appropriately at the Alhambra Theatre in London.

Ravel's most famous work, *Bolero*, his 'danse lascive', was first performed as a ballet in 1928 and danced by Ida Rubinstein. As he modestly said, it was based on folk-tunes of the 'usual Spanish-Arabic kind', and it was to achieve even greater success in orchestral performances. It was eagerly bought by Hollywood, in the wake of Valentino's passionate drama *Blood and Sand*, set in exotic Seville.

Falla met Federico García Lorca at Granada in 1919. Lorca had been born in 1898 at Fuente Vaqueros on the Duke of Wellington's estate. Poet, dramatist, musician, artist, he inspires more and more international respect as the years pass, not least because of his martyrdom in the Civil War. In some ways by the 1920s Ganivet's utopian dream in *Granada la*

Bella had come true, for Granada possessed by then a group of distinguished men passionately devoted to the arts and to the improvement of their city, including the artist Manuel Ortiz, the guitarist Andrés Segovia, the historian Gallego y Burín, the future editor of *El Defensor de Granada* Constantino Carnero, and Professor Fernando de los Ríos whose daughter later married Lorca's brother. Most of this circle assisted Falla and Lorca in the arranging of a *cante jondo* contest, held in 1922 in the Court of the Myrtles, when gypsy and country singers assembled in front of an audience dressed in early nineteenth-century costume. Other types of performances in succeeding years were the forerunners of the now yearly International Festival of Music and Dance that takes place in the Alhambra courts, the Generalife and the courtyard of the Palace of

78. *The dancer Josefa Vargas, known as 'Pepita'*

79. *A London Festival Ballet production of Falla's*
The Three Cornered Hat

Charles V. The Alhambra itself in the 1920s was already under a *patronato* or board of local trustees which appointed an architect in charge of restoration.

For all this Lorca criticized the philistinism of the majority of the Granadinos, particularly the bourgeois. By 1934, the year of his *Yerma*, and following *Blood Wedding* – full of deep passions and tragedy, and the all-important sense of honour, so truly of the South – he was the most famous living Spanish poet and dramatist. His *Romancero gitano* was partly based on Andalusian gypsies. He had published *El Poema de Cante Jondo* in 1931. When his *Mariana Pineda* opened in Granada he declared, 'If by the grace of God I become famous, half of that fame will belong to Granada which formed me and made me what I am.' 'Granada belongs to the whole world,' he was also fond of saying. 'We must love it in a European context.' His outspokenness made enemies, and when the Civil War broke out he incautiously returned from Madrid to Granada, where soon afterwards – at the height of his powers – he was brutally murdered by Nationalists, ironically in a place where Ibn al-Khatib, the greatest poet under the Nasrids, had had a palace.

After the Civil War, Falla left his Granada and went to live in Argentina, where he died. The number of executions in the city is not known, but 2137 people, including several intellectuals, are recorded as having been shot in the city cemetery, which lies on the road that passes the Alhambra and the Washington Irving Hotel; and 572 died in August 1936 alone, the month of Lorca's death. Granada had also been bombed by the Republicans, with many civilian casualties.

The Alhambra had been declared a national monument in 1870. Several years previously the convent of San Francisco had been closed; eventually this palace site, once the resting place of the bodies of Fernando and Isabel, became a popular hotel for artists and writers – now it is the Parador. Richard Ford's old home, the Casa Sánchez, was rescued and restored as the Partal Palace early in this century. The gardens of the Generalife were extended in the 1930s and the open-air theatre was built in 1951.

No longer does one approach the Hall of the Ambassadors by Ford's crumbling staircase. Not a tile is out of place on the roofs of the pavilions surrounding the Court of the Lions. The first of the names in modern times connected with the Alhambra's restoration and interpretation must be Leopoldo Torres Balbás. He was followed as architect in 1936 by Francisco Prieto-Moreno, in turn succeeded by his son Joaquín Prieto-Moreno. Other key figures have been Antonio Gallego y Burín, Luis Seco de Lucena, Manuel Gómez-Moreno, and Jesús Bermúdez Pareja, whose obsession with and love for the Alhambra have resulted in his affectionate nickname *el novio de la Alhambra*, the fiancé of the Alhambra; Seco de Lucena in particular has written a prodigious number of books and papers. In recent years we have had the work of Padre Dario Cabanelas and Antonio Fernández-Puertas, the present director of the

80. *Lorca in 1936, with Rafael Alberti, the poet, and 'La Argentinita'*

81 & 82. *The door of the Siete Suelos (Seven Floors) Tower was blown up by Napoleonic troops following their withdrawal. It has been rebuilt following exact documents and drawings existing at the time*

Museum. Then for years the great authority on the literature, art and civilization of Muslim Spain has been Emilio García Gómez, famous in Spain for his translations of Arabic poetry into rhythmical prose. The list would be a great deal longer if foreign names were added.

Among the sensational discoveries in the last decades has been a small piece of wood stuck in the ceiling of the Hall of the Ambassadors with Arabic writing giving the clue to the original colours. The whole ceiling has now been given a new significance. It is not just a marvel of mathematical precision, with its 8017 pieces, in attractively subdued tones. Once it was a glowing and brilliant firmament, with a design that follows chapter LXVII of the Koran. Here we have the seven heavens, with rows of stars and candles lighting the way to God in the centre, which would originally have been in white; out of this centre grew four trees of the Islamic paradise. The more the Alhambra is studied, the more apparent becomes its religious and cosmic significance – something that is lost, perhaps, to many casual Western visitors. The cupola of the Hall of the Two Sisters, for instance, is conceived as a dome of heaven: a rotating dome since the *muqarnas* or stalactites change colour constantly in the light. All this becomes clear through a poem by the eleventh-century Granadino poet Ibn Gabirol, in which an ideal palace, possibly an imaginary one, possibly the original Alhambra, is compared to the palace of Solomon.

Then there is the mystery of the Fountain of the Lions, which again seems to have associations with Solomon. Have these strange beasts been in this very spot ever since the eleventh century, or were they brought here from the palace in Granada that once belonged to Samuel Ibn Nagrella, the Jewish vizier to the Zirid king who ruled Granada after the fall of the Cordoban caliphate? And did the basin that is now lying in the Hall of the Abencerrajes really belong to this fountain?

The marble basin that is at present supported by the lions is decorated with a long poem by Ibn Zamrak. This poem is complex and full of the usual hyperboles, but fascinating on many levels, with its metaphor for water as a solid substance, and its references to war and victory. Throughout the Alhambra the poems and inscriptions provide clues to actual events and the original purposes of individual rooms. Nearly all the inscriptions had been copied out by Owen Jones and his French counterpart de Prangey in the 1840s, but they are now being meticulously analysed by Arabic scholars such as Padre Darió Cabanelas. At first reading they might appear all flattery, self-congratulation and piety, but deeper meanings become clear – for instance from an inscription in the Sala de la Barca which commemorates the capture of Algeciras in 1369 by Muhammed V. We know that the Hall of the Ambassadors was the throne room from the statement that 'My lord Yusuf the favourite of God has chosen me for his throne'. In the Generalife some of the remarks are charmingly naive: 'By God how beautiful is this niche placed on the right-hand of the king'; 'The merciful God will honour you, Moorish woman, if you serve the house of the king most pure'. Others are decidedly peremptory, as for example: 'Respect those who speak with beautiful words'; or again, 'Enter with modesty, talk with knowledge, be sparing with your words, and go in peace'. A reminder no doubt that the sultan was wishing to enjoy a rest in his summer palace and not waste time over visitors.

Domes of heaven, water, gardens: these are the three main images of the poems in the Alhambra. The association of gardens with paradise for the Arabs has its origins in the dream of an oasis, with fresh springs and lush foliage under the timeless, infinite sky. The Medina Azahara of the Caliph Abd el-Rahman III in tenth-century Córdoba had plenty of space for its gardens, but the Alhambra was a fortified city, and gardens had to be kept small, with miradors for the views stretching out across the Vega (the view from the Garden of Lindaraxa was blocked out by the additions by Charles V). The Generalife had more scope for an ambitious design, but again was limited by geography, though it also, incidentally, had orchards, vegetable gardens and grazing land for sheep. So much in the

83. *The dome above the prayer hall of the Madrasa, or university, built by Yusuf I*

Generalife has been altered over the Christian centuries – even in 1958 there was a small fire – but the restoration of the gardens and the recent addition of new ones (beautifully laid out) in the Hispano-Moresque tradition form a contrast to the stately enclosed courts below.

Yet, after wandering through avenues of cypresses and being dazzled by the sparkle of the arched fountains, and after listening to the murmur of the doves, and smelling the heavy scents of the glorious syringa, the honeysuckle and the roses, nothing seems more tranquil and more truly Moorish than the simple water staircase above the main palace buildings where the sultan would have cooled his wrists as he climbed under the bay trees to his oratory.

And the travellers? Books with titles like Penelope Chetwode's *Two Middle-Aged Ladies in Andalusia* are in the grand tradition, but Rose Macaulay's *Fabled Shore* is in the great tradition, the tradition of Gautier and Borrow. The Alhambra might have been described a thousand times before, but she does it all over again, brilliantly and wittily. Certainly in the time of Fernando VII travellers would have thought it inconceivable that lone Englishwomen would ever roam unprotected through

114

84. *The baths – a vaulted area with marble floors and ceramic tiles which were added by Charles V when the room was adapted for his personal use*

Andalusia. The intrepid Rose had actually been warned of bandits or 'maquis' in the mountains between Guadix and Granada, but took no notice. Since her day the fabled coastline has much altered, and scenically not for the better, but I am sure that in this age of the package tour, and when hundreds of thousands of people tramp through the Court of the Lions every year, her enthusiasm for Spain would not be altered.

It is noticeable that in the twenties and thirties the Alhambra lost ground in the favour of some travellers. Lytton Strachey dismissed it as 'sheer Earl's Court' and Augustus John seemed more affected by the gypsy girls. Mario Praz in *Unromantic Spain* is mocking and sarcastic, at the expense too of Washington Irving, but then he was a high priest of Neoclassicism. The Alhambra was an 'alien' world to him, with the 'perfection of cobwebs, beehives, snow-crystals, frost-flowers on the window'. To him the art of the Arabs, like the Irish art of illumination, had been born perfect and had crystallized; the Arab genius, abstract and mathematical, was constant with a multiplication of decorative devices. Superficially there is something in all this, though nobody would confuse the style of western Islam with that of Persia or even Egypt. Arab or Moorish architecture in Spain evolved gradually over the centuries; by the troubled fifteenth century it had reached a formula, and might well have developed further in times of peace. One also realizes that the Alhambra, built originally from such fragile substances, and with no expectation of a long life, inevitably with restoration has lost some of the patina of age, unlike for example the Taj Mahal. Poor materials magically converted into the material of art, archaism gilded with filigree: this, said García Gómez, was the real symbol of Nasrid civilization, hemmed in as it was on all sides, 'corroded by internal viruses, the slave of an irremediable past'. Anything at all cosmic about the Alhambra did not seem to impinge on Praz, neither did the importance of the calligraphic inscriptions; but he did remark on the 'subtlety' of the air and on the 'sublime' avenue of cypresses leading to the Generalife. The view from the Generalife reminded him of Florence, as it had Berenson, but he did not dwell otherwise on the views or on the landscapes framed in the Alhambra which are in reality part of the architecture itself, nor on the effects of water and changing light, all aimed at achieving perfect repose and intimacy. Again and again, those who know and love the Alhambra speak of the importance of seeing it at the sunset hour. As Marguerite Steen has said, 'A single daylight visit can give one but the shell of the mystery, the skeleton of an historical miracle which, whether one happens to like Moorish architecture or not, must leave a deep impression of awe and reverence within the soul.'

Lytton Strachey was on his way to see Gerald Brenan, who was living in the Alpujarras – that last, forlorn kingdom of Boabdil. Strachey hated it all, and warned the Woolfs against going there. 'It's Death. Death!' he

85 & 86. *Gypsies dancing for the author in the Sacromonte caves, Granada, 1954*

cried in his high-pitched voice. Gerald Brenan lived in his remote *pueblo* in that spectacular valley from 1920 to 1934. His book *South from Granada*, a small classic like Julian Pitt-Rivers' *People of the Sierra*, represents a different turn in the literature of Andalusia, being a study of local life at close quarters over many years. When Brenan told peasant neighbours, living in flat-roofed, whitewashed houses, that he had been in a war, they assumed that he had been fighting Moors. Were not all wars against the Moors?

Brenan went back in 1949 and wrote *The Face of Spain*. Neither of his books have much mention of the Alhambra. Perhaps he felt too much had already been said by others. He wrote of his search for Lorca's grave. Indeed anyone concerned with literature and coming to Granada for the first time, cannot escape the shadow of Lorca's death in that crystalline air. Marguerite Steen, Laurie Lee, V. S. Pritchett all experienced it and wrote about it.

The decade following the last war was a kind of golden age of travel literature in English about Spain and Andalusia, what with Rose Macaulay's and Brenan's books, Marguerite Steen's *Granada Window*, Laurie Lee's *A Rose for Winter*, V. S. Pritchett's *The Spanish Temper*. Both V. S. Pritchett and Laurie Lee found an affinity between the Alhambra and the desert and the steppes. The stalactite ceilings to Pritchett suggested not only the panoply of a tent but the greater panoply of the sky. Like Praz, he also saw in them the 'voluptuous dreams of mathematicians', as if one were looking up through the eyes of Arab astronomers to the 'suspended valleys of space'. To Laurie Lee the Alhambra was the 'home of pastoral kings, of poor shepherds raised to glory'. Both also wrote about the gypsies of Granada. In one splendid, vivid paragraph Laurie Lee sums them up: now they are a special caste, one of the aristocracies of Spain, and it is almost snobbish to claim descent from them. 'Indolent, insolent, rapacious and admired, they have annexed for themselves the country's folklore which they exploit with a brilliant and swashbuckling technique.' Out on a picnic he had watched gypsy girls dancing in an impromptu *zambra*, 'twirling among the cacti with a kind of intent and secret pleasure while their men sat round them on the rocks clapping and crying softly'. This is what most tourists would hope for, instead of perfunctory flamenco in a neon-lit cave hung with *kitsch* and copper pans.

In spite of the flummery and nonsense, the *kitsch*, and the clutching at arms and the begging outside the Alhambra and at San Nicolás, those caves of the Sacromonte are the heart of the gypsy world in Spain, and as a tourist in the caves you are aware that the gypsies are treating you as a big joke. The gypsies are very good at parodying themselves. If you are lucky enough to escape the tourist trap you might glimpse that extraordinary capacity they have, as Pritchett says, of conveying in their dancing 'the gradual crescendo of passion, the tightening of the nerves, the sense of sexual battle'. In that is their real art, and for once they might not be laughing at you; that, and in the trance-like singing of *cante jondo*, which is more Andalusian than gypsy, and which seems to echo through the centuries back to the old lost al-Andalus.

87. *A view of the Alhambra from the Albaicín, at sunset, with the Sierra Nevada in the background*

POSTSCRIPT

In Fez, after leaving Spain, I was told that there are still families of Andalusian descent who keep the keys of their houses in Granada. I also listened to music from the Jebala district in north-west Morocco which had an obvious Andalusian influence.

I had driven south through Tetouan and Chechaouen. Tetouan must have seemed a magic haven for those Moriscos and Jews who had reached it in the fifteenth century, with its river and fertile valley and the protecting mountains. It is pleasant to walk through the steep streets of the old town, among the blue-washed houses and twisted vines. There is still a Jewish quarter, and there are remains of a castle and walls. Yet its atmosphere is neither Moroccan nor Spanish; it is unlike anywhere else in the country. Chechaouen, on the other hand, with its fantastic multi-coloured tiled roofs and all its flowers, reminded me much more of Andalusia. The light too is rather like Granada's.

For years I had longed to stay in the Palais Jamaï Hotel and now I felt able to afford it. The original building was the nineteenth-century palace of a vizier. It stands above the basin of Fez al-Bali, old Fez, and has a large garden with enormous palms swathed in ivy where pigeons nest. I had hoped to find some equivalent of the Alhambra in the city but the important buildings remaining from the Marinid period, coinciding with the Nasrids of Granada, were the *medrasa* or theological colleges, and in only one of these may a non-Muslim enter: the largest, the Medersa 'bn Inaria, buried in a maze of confusing alleys and built in the 1350s, just before the Court of the Lions. Although richly coloured, it is a much more austere building than any of those in the Alhambra, more virile and as one would expect more serious, impressive especially for the wooden grilles between the columns, and with little rooms for students above. It also has a graceful minaret.

I looked down on this minaret from the Palais Jamaï. There was a hum in the great city and lights were appearing, as the grey houses turned mauve and then pink. Then suddenly the muezzin was called, first from one minaret, then another, then another. I imagined myself standing – no, I imagined Boabdil standing, for the last time in his Alhambra, at the slender window beneath the Tower of Comares, and hearing the same call to evening prayer from the mosque on the Albaicín where the Church of San Salvador now stands.

Ill-fated indeed was the man who lost all that.

THE NASRID SULTANS OF GRANADA

MUHAMMED I (IBN AL-AHMAR), 1237–1273 The Alcazaba rebuilt, Gate of the Weapons

MUHAMMED II, 1273–1302

MUHAMMED III, 1302–1309 Palace of the Partal, west façade of Wine Gate

NASR, 1309–1314

ISMAIL I, 1314–1325 Mexuar, Baths, Generalife restored

MUHAMMED IV, 1325–1333

YUSUF I, 1333–1354 Hall of the Ambassadors, Tower of the Captive, Gate of Justice

MUHAMMED V, 1354–1359 and 1362–1391 Palace of the Lions, Sala de la Barca, façade of Comares

ISMAIL II, 1359–1360

MUHAMMED VI (EL REY BERMEYO), 1360–1362

YUSUF II, 1391–1392

MUHAMMED VII, 1392–1408 Tower of the Infantas

YUSUF III, 1408–1417

MUHAMMED VIII (EL PEQUENO) 1417–1419 and 1427–1429

MUHAMMED IX (EL ZURDO), 1419–1427, 1430–1431, 1432–1445, 1447–1453

YUSUF IV, 1432–1445

MUHAMMED X (EL COJO), 1445–1447

YUSUF V, 1445–1446

MUHAMMED XI (EL CHIQUITO), 1448–1454

SAAD, 1454–1462 and 1464

ALI (MULEY HASAN), 1464–1485

MUHAMMED XII (BOABDIL, EL REY CHICO), 1482–1492

MUHAMMED XIII (EL ZAGAL), 1485–1487

KINGS OF CASTILE

FERNANDO III (EL SANTO), 1217–1252 After 1230 also King of León
ALFONSO X (EL SABIO), 1252–1284
SANCHO IV (EL VALIENTE), 1284–1295
FERNANDO IV (EL EMPLAZADO), 1295–1312
ALFONSO XI, 1312–1350
PEDRO (EL CRUEL), 1350–1369
ENRIQUE II (DE TRASTAMARA), 1369–1379
JUAN I, 1379–1390
ENRIQUE III (EL DOLIENTE), 1390–1406
JUAN II, 1406–1454
ENRIQUE IV (EL IMPOTENTE), 1454–1474
ISABEL I (LA CATOLICA), 1474–1504 Married to Fernando II of Aragon
JUANA (LA LOCA), 1504–1516
(Philip of Burgundy, Regent as FELIPE I, 1504–1506)
(Fernando II of Aragon, Regent as FERNANDO V, 1506–1516)

NOTES ON THE ILLUSTRATIONS

1. The Alhambra gardens. and the Tower of the Captive where traditionally Isabel de Solís was imprisoned. (*Werner Forman*)
2. Plan of the Alhambra, drawn by David Eccles.
3. The Alhambra from the Tower of San Cristóbal. Drawing by Richard Ford, 1833. (*Sir Brinsley Ford*)
4. Muslim warriors defending a fortress. Detail from one of the *Commentarios al Apocalipsis del Beato de Liebana*, a tenth-century Mozarabic manuscript in the Museo Catedral in Gerona. (*Arxiu Mas*)
5. The approach to Granada. A sketch by Richard Ford, 1831. (*Sir Brinsley Ford*)
6. The interior of the mosque at Córdoba, begun in 785. (*Werner Forman*)
7. The dome of the Mihrab in the mosque at Córdoba, added by Hakim I in the tenth century. (*Werner Forman*)
8. El Cid. A contemporary woodcut. (*Mansell Collection*)
9. Alfonso VI. Portrait from his tomb in the cathedral of Santiago de Compostela, Coruña. (*Arxiu Mas*)

88 & 89. *llustrations from the Byzantine chronicle of John Skylitzes showing early Muslim conquests in Messina, Sicily*

10. Moorish warriors of different tribes. Detail from one of the *Commentarios al Apocalipsis del Beato de Liebana*, in the Biblioteca Nacional in Madrid, eleventh century. (*Arxiu Mas*)

11. The Giralda in Seville. Drawing by John F. Lewis (1805–76). (*Sir Brinsley Ford*)

12. James I of Aragón (1213–1276) with his knights. Detail from a fresco of the Conquest of Mallorca, 1229, in the Palacio Berenguer de Aguilar, Museo de Arte Catalán, Barcelona. (*Werner Forman*)

13. The Alcazaba and the Tower of the Siete Suelos, or Seven Floors. Gouache by Richard Ford from a sketch made in 1831. (*Sir Brinsley Ford*)

14. Muslim soldiers going to war. Detail from a fresco of the Conquest of Mallorca in the Palacio Berenguer de Aguilar. (*Werner Forman*)

15. Alfonso X at court. From a thirteenth-century manuscript in the Library of the Escorial. (*Michael Holford*)

16. The Court of the Alberca, later called the Myrtles. Wash drawing by David Roberts in the Pilkington Collection at Eton College. (*Courtauld Institute of Art*)

17. The horseshoe arch leading into the Cuarto Dorado. (*Werner Forman*)

18. The Comares tower reflected in the waters of the Court of the Myrtles. (*Werner Forman*)

19. The Court of the Lions. Drawing by Harriet Ford (1806–36). (*Sir Brinsley Ford*)

20. Moors playing chess. From a manuscript in the Library of the Escorial. (*Michael Holford*)

21. Detail of plaster work in the Alhambra. (*Werner Forman*)

22. The window of the mirador, looking out over the Garden of Lindaraxa. (*Werner Forman*)

23. A marble ablution tank with a carved animal design. Granada, eleventh century. (*Werner Forman*)

24. The Battle of La Higueruela. Fresco by Fabricio Castello and Nicolás Granello in the Sala de Batallas in the Monasterio del Escorial, 1589. (*Oroñoz*)

25 & 26. The battle of Alhama and the surrender of Alora. From a series of relief carvings in the choir stalls of Toledo cathedral, showing the various stages of the Reconquest. (*Arxiu Mas*)

27. Portraits of Fernando and Isabel taken from a contemporary document in the Universidad Privilegio in Valladolid. (*Arxiu Mas*)

28. A ceremonial Muslim sword with a brass hilt. Granada, fourteenth century. (*Werner Forman*)

29 & 30. Attempted assassination of the Catholic Kings, and the surrender of Granada. Two relief carvings from a series in the choir stalls of Toledo cathedral. (*Arxiu Mas*)

31. A detail from the Battle of La Higueruela. A fresco by Fabricio Castello and Nicolás Granello in the Sala de Batallas in the Monasterio del Escorial, 1589. (*Oroñoz*)

32. Knights wooing, hawking, feasting and jousting. From a fifteenth-century Catalan manuscript, Matfre Ermengaud's *Breviari d'Amor*. (*Trustees of the British Museum*)

33. The entry of the Catholic Kings into Granada, 1492. Polychrome relief in the Capilla Real in Granada cathedral. (*Oroñoz*)

34. A fortified town in the Granada area. Painting by Soloman Caesar Malan, *c.* 1830. (*Mary Evans Picture Library*)

35. Detail from a fresco of the Conquest of Mallorca in the Palacio Berenguer de Aguilar. (*Werner Forman*)

36. The sultans of Granada. Painting on the ceiling of the Hall of Justice in the Court of the Lions. (*Oroñoz*)
37. *Auto da fe*. Painting by Pedro Berruguete, *c*. 1490s. (*Museo del Prado, Madrid*)
38. A street in the Albaicín. (*El Estado de Turismo, Madrid*)
39. The Dar-al-Horra, last of the Nasrid palaces, *c*. 1450. (*Werner Forman*)
40. A cobbled street in the Albaicín. Photograph by K. Hielscher in *Picturesque Spain*, published by T. Fisher Unwin Limited, 1922.
41. The Alhambra vase. Fourteenth-century lustre-ware vase, over four feet tall, thought to be manufactured in Málaga. In the Museo Nacional de Arte Hispanomusulman, Alhambra. (*Werner Forman*)
42. The Alcaicería, the old silk market. (*Werner Forman*)
43. The tomb of Fernando and Isabel in Granada cathedral. Drawing by David Roberts in the Victoria and Albert Museum. (*Victoria and Albert Museum*)
44. Ceramic tile, showing the arms of the Nasrid sultans entwined in the foliage. Fourteenth-century tile, probably from the Alhambra, now in the National Museum of Archaeology, Madrid. (*Werner Forman*)
45. Red and gold silk, woven in Granada in the fifteenth century. From the National Museum of Archaeology, Madrid. (*Werner Forman*)
46. Philip II. Full-length portrait in the Museo del Prado, Madrid
47. Don John of Austria. Painting by Alonso Sánchez Coello, *c*. 1570. (*Museo del Prado, Madrid*)
48. The fountain in the Court of the Lions. The lions are thought to be Byzantine in origin. (*Werner Forman*)
49. The Patio de la Sultana in the Generalife, laid down in the fourteenth century. (*Werner Forman*)
50. A priest trying to convert the Moors to Christianity. Woodcut from the title-page of *Improbatio Alcorani* by Ricoldus de Montecrucis, *c*. 1500. (*Trustees of the British Museum*)
51. Silk woven in Granada in the thirteenth or fourteenth centuries. (*Werner Forman*)
52. The Darro river flowing through Granada. Engraving by Gustave Doré, *c* 1870. (*Mary Evans Picture Library*)
53. The Court of the Lions, showing the fountain and water courses. (*Werner Forman*)
54. Families living and working in the Tower of the Infantas. Water-colour by John F. Lewis, 1833. (*Sir Brinsley Ford*)
55. 'Modern Christians in the palaces of the ancient Moorish kings.' Satirical engraving by Gustave Doré, *c* 1870. (*Mary Evans Picture Library*)
56. The Casa Sánchez in the Alhambra. Water-colour by John F. Lewis, 1832. (*Sir Brinsley Ford*)
57. View of the Comares tower and the Hall of the Ambassadors from the Tocador de la Reina. Coloured drawing by Richard Ford, 1831. (*Sir Brinsley Ford*)
58. Washington Irving. Engraving in the Mansell Collection
59. A chat round the brasero. Painting by John Phillip (1817–67) in the Guildhall Art Gallery. (*Bridgeman Art Library*)
60. José María, the bandit. Drawing by John F. Lewis (1805–76). (*Sir Brinsley Ford*)
61. The apartments above the Mexuar patio. Drawing by Harriet Ford, 1831. (*Sir Brinsley Ford*)
62. Puerto de Arenas, on the road to Granada from Jaén. Water-colour and gouache by Richard Ford, (1796–1858). (*Sir Brinsley Ford*)

63. Three studies of Richard Ford in Spanish dress. Painting by Joaquín Becquer (1805–41). (*Sir Brinsley Ford*)

64. Harriet Ford in the dress of a *maja de Sevilla*. Painting by R. R. Reinagle (1775–1851) after a print by J. F. Lewis. Lewis's print was probably taken from a drawing by this artist. (*Sir Brinsley Ford*)

65. The pool of the Partal and the Tower of Las Damas. The Casa Sánchez, where the Fords lodged in 1833, was restored to its former magnificence at the beginning of this century. (*Werner Forman*)

66. Portrait of San Fernando. Painting by Murillo in the Museo del Prado. (*Museo del Prado, Madrid*)

67 & 68. Designs from the capitals of columns in the Court of the Lions. From *The Alhambra* by Albert F. Calvert, 1904.

69 & 70. Designs from arches and panels in the Alhambra for *The Grammar of Ornament* by Owen Jones, 1868.

71. A priest and majos admiring the Alhambra vase. Engraving by Gustave Doré, *c* 1870. (*Mary Evans Picture Library*)

72. The Hall of the Abencerrajes. Painting by David Roberts in the Laing Art Gallery, Newcastle-upon-Tyne. (*Laing Art Gallery*)

73 & 74. Two views of the Alhambra Anastatica in Italy. (*Franco Maria Ricci Editore*)

75. Albert F. Calvert in Moorish dress posing for the frontispiece of his book, *The Alhambra*, published in 1904.

76. Manuel de Falla. Drawing by Picasso. (*Arxiu Mas*)

77. Federico García Lorca. Painting by Gregorio Prieto. (*Arxiu Mas*)

78. Josefa Vargas, known as 'Pepita'. Painting by Antonio de Esquivel in the collection of the Duquesa de Alba. (*Arxiu Mas*)

79. Scene from the London Festival Ballet production of Manuel de Falla's *The Three Cornered Hat*. (*Mike Davis*)

80. Newspaper photograph of Federico García Lorca in 1936, the year of his death, with Rafael Alberti and 'La Argentinita'. (*Arxiu Mas*)

81 & 82. Two photographs showing restoration work on the Tower of the Siete Suelos, or Seven Floors. (*Joaquín and Carmen Prieto-Moreno*)

83. The prayer hall of the Madrasa, built by Yusuf I in 1349. (*Werner Forman*)

84. The marble floors and ceramic tiles of the baths. (*Werner Forman*)

85 & 86. Gypsies dancing for the author in Granada. (*Raleigh Trevelyan*)

87. Panoramic view of the Alhambra at sunset with the Sierra Nevada in the background (*Werner Forman*)

88 & 89. The siege of Messina in Sicily. These two illustrations from the eleventh-century Byzantine chronicle of John Skylitzes give a splendid impression of the force of the Islamic invasion of Europe in the ninth century. (*Werner Forman*)

BIBLIOGRAPHY

Arié, Rachel. *L'Espagne Musulmane au temps des Nasrides*. Paris 1973.

Ars Hispaniae. Vol IV. Madrid 1949.

Arts Council of Great Britain. *The Arts of Islam*. Catalogue. London 1976.

Bargebuhr, Frederick P. The Alhambra Palace of the Eleventh Century. *Journal of the Warburg and Courtauld Institute*, vol XIX. London 1956.

Baticle, Jeannine, and Marinas, Cristina. *La Galerie espagnole de Louis Philippe au Louvre*. Catalogue. Paris 1981.

Bermúdez Pareja, Jesús. *El Generalife*. Granada 1974.

Boase, Roger. *The Troubadour Revival*. London 1978.

Brett, Michael and Forman, Werner. *The Moors*. London 1980.

Cabanelas Rodríguez, Darío. La Antigua Policroma del Techo de Comares. *Cuadernos de la Alhambra 8*. Granada 1972.

Calvert, Albert F. *The Alhambra*. London and Liverpool 1904.

Cheyne, Anwar G. *Muslim Spain*. Minneapolis 1974.

Dickie, James. The Alhambra: Some Reflections. *AARP 16*. London 1979.

Fernández-Puertas, Antonio. *Map and Guide of the Alhambra*. Madrid 1979.

Ford, Richard. *Granada*. Granada 1955.

Ford, Richard. *Murray's Hand-Book for Spain*. Revised edition. London 1892.

Gallego y Burín, Antonio. *Guía de Granada*. Granada 1946.

Gallego Morell, Antonio. *Ganivet y Granada*. Granada 1975.

García Gómez, Emilio. *Cinco Poetas Musulmanes*. Madrid 1944.

—— and Bermúdez Pareja, Jesús. *La Alhambra: La Casa Real*. Granada 1966.

Gibb, H. A. R. *Arabic Literature*. Oxford 1963.

Gibson, Ian. *The Death of Lorca*. London 1973.

Gómez-Moreno y Martinez, Manuel. *Guía de Granada*. Granada 1892.

Grabar, Oleg. *The Alhambra*. London 1978.

Guiterman, Helen. *David Roberts, R. A*. London 1981.

Hurtado de Mendoza, Diego. *The War in Granada*. Translated by Martin Shuttleworth. London 1982.

Irving, Washington. *The Alhambra*. Introduced by Elizabeth Robins Pennell. London 1896.

—— *Chronicle of the Conquest of Granada*. Revised edition. London 1850.

Jones, Terry. *Chaucer's Knight*. London 1980.

Ladero Quesada, Miguel Angel. *Granada*. Madrid 1969.

Lévi-Provencal, E. *La Civilización Arabe en España*. Madrid 1953.

Lipschutz, Ilse Hempel. *Spanish Painting and the French Romantics*. Cambridge, Mass. 1972.

Lomax, Derek W. *The Reconquest of Spain*. London 1978.

Menendez Pidal, Ramón. *Historia de España*. Vol XVII. Madrid 1969.

Ministero de Cultura, Dirección General de Bellas Artes, Archivos y Bibliotecas. *Imagen Romántica de España*. Catalogue 2 vols. Madrid 1981

Molina Fajardo, Eduardo. *Sacromonte Gitano*. Granada 1971.

O'Callaghan, Joseph F. *A History of Medieval Spain*. Ithaca and London 1975.

Orozco Díaz, Manuel. *Falla y Granada*. Granada 1976.

Pahissa, Jaime. *Manuel de Falla*. London 1954.

Peers, E. Allison, ed. *Spain: A Companion to Spanish Studies*. London 1956.

Prescott, William H. *History of the Reign of Ferdinand and Isabella*. Revised edition. London 1886.

Prieto-Moreno, Francisco. *Los Jardines de Granada*. Madrid 1983.

Read, Jan. *The Moors in Spain and Portugal*. London 1974.

Robertson, Ian. *Los Curiosos Impertinentes*. Madrid 1975.

Russell, P. E., ed. *Spain: A Companion to Spanish Studies*. London 1973.

Said, Edward W. *Orientalism*. London 1978.

Seco de Lucena Paredes, Luis. *Granada*. León 1980.

—— *El Libro de la Alhambra*. León 1975.

Soria, Andrés. *García Lorca y Granada*. Granada 1978.

Stewart, Desmond. *The Alhambra*. New York 1974.

Torres Balbás, Leopoldo. *La Alhambra y el Generalife*. Madrid 1953.

Watt, William Montgomery. *A History of Islamic Spain*. Edinburgh 1965.

Watts, Henry Edward. *Spain*. London 1893.

Wildenstein & Co. *Richard Ford in Spain*. Catalogue. London 1974.

Wishaw, Bernhard and Ellen. *Arabic Spain*. London 1912.